Business Intelligence for Small and Medium-Sized Enterprises

Business Intelligence for Small and Medium-Sized Enterprises

An Agile Roadmap toward Business Sustainability

Lila Rao-Graham, Maurice L. McNaughton, and Gunjan Mansingh

CRC Press
Taylor & Francis Group
Boca Raton London New York

CRC Press is an imprint of the
Taylor & Francis Group, an **informa** business

AN AUERBACH BOOK

CRC Press
Taylor & Francis Group
6000 Broken Sound Parkway NW, Suite 300
Boca Raton, FL 33487-2742

First issued in paperback 2022

© 2020 by Taylor & Francis Group, LLC
CRC Press is an imprint of Taylor & Francis Group, an Informa business

No claim to original U.S. Government works

ISBN 13: 978-1-03-247540-0 (pbk)
ISBN 13: 978-1-138-58421-1 (hbk)
ISBN 13: 978-0-429-31637-1 (ebk)

DOI: 10.1201/9780429316371

Publisher's Note
The publisher has gone to great lengths to ensure the quality of this reprint but points out that some imperfections in the original copies may be apparent.

**Visit the Taylor & Francis Web site at
http://www.taylorandfrancis.com**

**and the CRC Press Web site at
http://www.crcpress.com**

The measure of intelligence is the ability to change

Albert Einstein

Contents

PART II NAVIGATING THE AGILE BI PROCESS

Foreword

Drs Lila Rao-Graham, Gunjan Mansingh and Maurice L. McNaughton, my illustrious coconspirators in the quest for excellence in the provision of high quality and effective Information Systems applications, particularly for small and medium enterprises, have undertaken an enormously important assignment: the writing of a book on Business Intelligence (BI) with particular emphasis on its utilization in Small and Medium–sized Enterprises (SME's), targeting owners, decision-makers, and workers as well as academics and students. It is a project that I am extraordinarily proud to be associated with for several reasons, but particularly because of my long association with all three authors, as former protégés who are now full-fledged colleagues, confidantes and collaborators in the quest to advance knowledge in the often-discussed, but not well-understood subject area of the application of Business Intelligence (BI) in SME's. The application of BI in SMEs requires a solid understanding of the nuances as well as the peculiarities of these enterprises in comparison to their larger counterparts. It is an understanding that the authors have amply demonstrated in this exceptional publication.

But I can think of no better group to address the peculiar issues that are associated with this demanding undertaking than this super experienced team of Drs Rao, Mansingh and McNaughton. They have invested heavily in a deep understanding of these issues and have spent a large part of their scholarly pursuits studying, assimilating and disseminating knowledge in the areas of Business Analytics and SMEs. This is not a declaration I make lightly; I have observed their impressive work in this area close up, with great admiration. Dr Rao has undertaken extensive work in BI, Data Quality and Decision Support Systems with particular focus on assisting organizations leverage the value from data through effective decision-making. Dr McNaughton runs UWI Mona's Centre of Excellence for IT-enabled Business Innovation with particular emphasis on Small and Medium Enterprises and Dr. Mansingh has focused her research and interest largely on Business Intelligence, Data Mining, Decision Support Systems and Knowledge Management.

The notion of BI has evolved over several years as organizations have extended their online transaction processing (OLTP) capabilities and applications to support their routine operations and established the capability to extract internal and external data from a variety of sources to specifically obtain intelligence about non-routine and often less-structured arrangements, through Online analytical processing (OLAP). BI therefore refers to applications and technologies that are used to gather, provide access to, and analyze data and information about the operations of an organization, with the capability of providing comprehensive insights into the more volatile factors affecting the business and its operations, thereby facilitating enhanced decision-making quality and contributing to the creation of business value. Larger and more sophisticated organizations have long been exploiting these capabilities. This work seeks to provide guidance to SMEs to replicate this experience and is the unique contribution of *Business Intelligence for SME's: An Agile Roadmap toward Business Sustainability*.

The authors have done an excellent job in explicating this evolution and how the various terms we have used along the way to describe the migration toward the exceedingly important organizational notions and use of the data and information. They possess the skills and experience to not merely seek out operational efficiencies but, on a hugely different magnitude, to extract intelligence from the information and data available to organizations. They are quick to point out that successful BI implementations have generated significant increases in revenue and cost savings, however, the failure rates are also very high. But more importantly the emphasis of this publication (which is the huge selling point) is that these capabilities are not the exclusive purview of large organizations, but may yet become the saving grace of SMEs. They have begun to make extensive use of these techniques to ensure the kind of agility that will endow them with the organizational capability to sense and respond to opportunities and threats in an increasing dynamic business environment – an environment in which smaller organizations could have an increasingly larger role by establishing, among other capabilities, the agility to leverage internal and external data and information assets to enhance competitiveness by having a comprehensive understanding of a process that will ultimately be the "key" to an agile roadmap for business sustainability – the authors have emphasized this beautifully throughout this publication.

Drs Rao, Mansingh and McNaughton underscore the point that, in the not too distant past, there was the misapprehension that BI is for large, resource-intensive enterprises, however, this is no longer the case. SMEs have a natural latent agility that can only be enhanced by the appropriate application of BI. In addition, they have introduced a process model born out of their experiences and insights with real-world examples that is a must read for SMEs. This model, and the critical success factors for their implementation, can be adapted by both practitioners and researchers, in their quest to acquire greater agility through strategic BI. The authors, recognizing the fact that several organizations have invested in the BI tools and technologies without the appropriate focus on the prerequisites and processes that are required to maximize the benefits, present a process to assist organizations in harnessing the returns from their BI investments. They also provide recommendations to assist SMEs in identifying and implementing their BI projects; not in a generic manner but conditioned by the peculiarities of their focused needs and capabilities.

Traditional BI approaches have often been considered unsuitable for SMEs and were once positioned as the strategic apparatus of larger and more resourced organizations. The authors effectively contradict this fiction and identify the several opportunities and approaches that are available to SMEs in this domain and provide real and excellent examples of how these organizations can identify, understand and apply appropriate BI approaches to their peculiar benefit.

The book is tremendously well organized. It effectively introduces the subjects of BI and the concepts of agility and their importance and traces the evolution of the subject area. Commendably, it provides an extremely useful discourse on strategies for enhancing, as well as barriers to, the adoption of ICT in SMEs. It provides an excellent (must read) overview of Agile Process Model for Strategic BI, and then tackles the important issue of how to assess Information Maturity. The discussion of how to evaluate business capabilities and gaps in strategic BI is simply excellent. There is also a must-read explication of important aspects of BI, including the exceedingly important notions of data governance, data integration and data services and quality management. This unusual volume closes with two extraordinarily important discussions: how to develop a roadmap for strategic BI and how to measure the success of BI initiatives.

This book is a gem! It is a conclusive treatise that BI and indeed data analytics are extraordinarily significant artilleries for SMEs and certainly not the exclusive apparatus of the corporate world. The authors have convincingly presented a superb case for the use of these powerful techniques that have the capability to assist smaller organizations to reap the enormous BI benefits that have long accrued to their corporate counterparts; allowing them to take targeted action to improve decision-making about their operational performance, reduce risk and identify opportunities for improvement, and plan for the future.

Evan W. Duggan, Ph.D.
Former Visiting Professor at the University
of Alabama in Birmingham
Former Dean of the Faculty of Social Sciences and
Professor of MIS at UWI Mona, Jamaica

Authors

Lila Rao-Graham is the deputy executive director and a senior lecturer in Information Systems at the Mona School of Business and Management, The University of the West Indies (UWI), Jamaica. She holds a PhD in Information Systems from The University of the West Indies. She lectures courses in Database Management Systems, Enterprise Data Management and Business Analytics.

Her research interests include Business Intelligence, Data Quality. Knowledge Management and Decision Support Systems.

Maurice L. McNaughton is the director of the Centre of Excellence for IT-enabled Innovation at the Mona School of Business and Management, The University of the West Indies (UWI), Jamaica. He holds a PhD in Decision Sciences from Georgia State University. He lectures courses in Modelling and Decision Support Systems; IT Economics; IT Governance and Strategic use of ICT.

His research interest spans the domain of emerging Open ICT ecosystems, and includes Open Source Software, Open/Big Data, Mobile and Cloud Computing.

Gunjan Mansingh is head of the Department and a Senior Lecturer at the Department of Computing, The University of the West Indies (UWI), Mona, Jamaica. She holds a PhD in Information Systems from The University of the West Indies. She lectures courses in Business Intelligence, Programming, Artificial Intelligence and Knowledge Discovery and Analytics.

Her research interests include Business Intelligence, Data Mining, Machine Leaning, Decision Support Systems, Knowledge Management and Expert Systems.

INTRODUCTION

Conceptions of Agility and Business Intelligence for SMEs

In the new world, it is not the big fish which eats the small fish, it's the fast fish which eats the slow fish.

Klaus Schwab

Digital Business Trends

Digital is rapidly becoming the dominant mode of interaction for commercial, social and economic activity, resulting in the emergence of what is often referred to as the Digital economy. Data has been described as the oil that fuels the Digital economy and an organization's ability to *collect, manage, use and generate insights* from Data for a variety of business scenarios and activities has become an essential capability. With the increasingly digital nature of business interactions, the ability of organizations to exploit distinctive data assets and analytics capabilities presents enormous opportunities for increased operational efficiency, greater customer intimacy and improved service delivery and will be critical to their ability to utilize information as a competitive weapon.

Davenport and Harris (2007) describe many exemplars of organizations that make widespread use of business analytics and data assets to create significant value for them, allow them to leapfrog over competitors who possess more traditional advantages of size, financial assets and physical infrastructure. The well-known example of Netflix, which began as a start-up founded on the premise of using analytics as the basis of competition and was able to dominate and eventually clobber the much larger, more established Blockbuster, should inspire many small businesses to embrace Klaus Schwab's oft-cited mantra: *"In the new world, it is not the big fish which eats the small fish, it's the fast fish which eats the slow fish"*. In other words, **size doesn't matter, agility does!**

Conceptions of Agility

Being Agile has become a recurrent theme in the modern business discourse, and many executives now see this as an increasingly important organizational capability necessary to be able to compete effectively in the Digital economy. Business agility is generally defined as *"the capacity of firms to sense and respond readily to opportunities and threats in a dynamic business environment"*. However, there are several identifiable dimensions to Agility within the organizational context:

Firstly, Agility has its roots in the Software Development discipline, where the *Agile Manifesto* prescribes the following key principles to improve success rates in project implementation:

- *Incremental delivery*: Deliver functionality in increments with the involved customer validating and specifying the requirements to be included in each increment.
- *People not process*: Empower the project team and allow team members to develop their own ways of working without prescriptive processes.
- *Embrace change*: Expect the business requirements to evolve and design the solution to accommodate changes.
- *Maintain simplicity*: Focus on simplicity in both the product being developed and in the development process. Wherever possible, actively work to eliminate complexity from the system.

These practices are not exclusive to software development, but are generally applicable to any kind of business activity.

Secondly, modern Human Resource practitioners increasingly embrace *Agile* organizational behaviors such as:

- Encouraging a fail-fast, learn-fast culture.
- Talent recruitment through social media platforms such as LinkedIn and Facebook.
- Flexi-work policies that allow employees to *"work when, how, where you want"*.
- Building a workplace environment and culture to attract millennials and digital natives.

- Adopting a self-service paradigm for human resource services delivery.

Thirdly, an increasing number of digital transformational initiatives are beginning to manifest themselves in organizations that are seeking to increase *Operational Agility* by employing modern technology platforms to digitize core enterprise work infrastructure and processes such as customer-facing channels, order fulfillment, supply chain relationship management and product and/or service innovation.

Ultimately, business agility is seen as a leadership imperative and requires executives to:

- Embrace dynamic, adaptive business models;
- Exhibit entrepreneurial alertness that enables the firm to explore its marketplace, detect areas of marketplace ignorance and seize on opportunities for action;
- Adopt a *visionary* perspective through strategic foresighting and analytic-driven insight;
- Lead and inspire the organizational culture change required for digital transformation.

Organizations that aspire to this kind of transformational culture, aptitude and agility will need to develop the analytic orientation and business intelligence capabilities similar to those of the Analytic Competitors described by Davenport and Harris (2007).

Business Intelligence as an Enabler of Agility

Business Intelligence, Data Analytics, Business Analytics and Data Mining are often used interchangeably in the academic and trade literature as well as by practitioners. For the purposes of this book, we treat Business Intelligence (BI) as an umbrella term for a wide range of processes, tools, techniques and capabilities whereby organizations create business value from their data assets.

This definition of Business Intelligence offered by Forrester (2014) is:

> …an approach that combines processes, methodologies, organizational structure, tools, and technologies that enable strategic, tactical, and operational decision-makers to be more flexible and more responsive to the fast pace of changes to business and regulatory requirements.

This definition situates BI as an organizational capability that enables business agility. BI has become a strategic initiative and is now recognized by business and technology leaders as instrumental in driving business effectiveness and innovation. Companies that have been successful in BI implementations have seen their investments in BI generate increases in revenue and produce cost savings that realize significant returns on their investment (ROI). However, many other organizational BI initiatives struggle through a myriad of technology platforms, reporting tools and localized data sources that fail to deliver the consistent information required to drive value-added and timely executive decision-making.

The design and implementation of the classical data warehouse architecture that underpins many BI Systems can be technically and financially daunting for organizations without the requisite technical resources. Smaller organizations in particular are often challenged by the complexity and resource requirements of traditional BI solutions.

SMEs, Business Intelligence and Agility

Does this mean that the potential operational efficiency improvements, customer intimacy and competitive benefits associated with BI and business analytics have become even more inaccessible to small businesses that are limited by resource and expertise constraints?

Definitely not! Indeed, we argue that perhaps more so than any other enterprise information system, BI gives SMEs the opportunity to combine business agility with their natural flexibility, to create a distinctive competitive advantage that typically eludes larger organizations confined by more formal structures and bureaucracy.

The importance of the small and medium enterprise (SME) sector as a principal contributor to the economic well-being of most societies is acknowledged for both developed and developing economies. SMEs are often both the product and the producers of entrepreneurial creativity and, in most countries, have become progressively important pillars of economic stability. Their actual and potential contributions to innovation, economic growth, employment and the diversification of productive endeavors are well documented.

Notwithstanding the acknowledged importance of the SME sector, many such organizations face a variety of challenges contingent on their size, when contemplating the implementation of advanced ICTs such as BI. These inherent characteristics often include:

- Limited technology competencies and awareness of strategic ICT value opportunities.
- Lack of the implementation skills and absorptive capacity to effectively deploy ICT-enabled solutions.
- Typically, a single owner-manager who is the principal decision-maker, burdened with multiple responsibilities.
- Heavy dependency on external technology advice through intermediaries or vendors.

As a result, traditionally, SMEs have not done well in the adoption of Enterprise ICTs as enablers of business innovation often limiting their efforts to basic operational and transactional ICT systems.

Fortunately, the availability of modern cloud computing infrastructure and previously prohibitive (due to cost and complexity) enterprise applications through software-as-a-service have made a range of modern ICT capabilities accessible and affordable to even the smallest organizations. Small business innovators can now access and use the most advanced BI solutions for a modest monthly expense and thus give themselves a fighting chance in the globally competitive business landscape.

While access to the technology addresses an important barrier, it alone is insufficient to harness the benefits of BI. SMEs need a systematic, yet practical approach that allows them to discover value-adding opportunities for charting their own customized roadmap toward realizing the strategic benefits of BI. That is the underlying premise for this book.

About this Book

This book was conceptualized out of the authors' combined years of experience in research, education and consulting with large and small organizations in the application of ICTs to enable business innovation. These engagements have forged a conviction that small businesses today have an unprecedented opportunity to embrace and harness modern ICTs, in particular, BI, to unleash and amplify the natural entrepreneurial spirit and nimbleness of their businesses.

The book is based on the *Agile Integrated Methodology for Strategic Business Intelligence (AIMS-BI)*, a highly adaptable process model for implementing BI that was formulated based on the authors' collective experiences. It provides SME business and technology managers with a practical guide and supporting toolkit for the effective implementation of enterprise business intelligence systems.

The book is structured in three sections:

Part I: BI Landscape – Opportunities for SMEs, examines the evolving digital economy, implications for business and the role that BI and analytics can play in helping SMEs to navigate the emerging opportunities and challenges. It introduces the AIMS-BI methodology as a practical guide to navigate this landscape.

Part II: Navigating the Agile BI Process, describes the stages and activities in the AIMS-BI methodology and details not just *what* should be done but also *how to do it*. The procedures are supported by examples and recommendations for less resource intensive options that make BI generally accessible for SMEs with limited financial and technical capacity.

Part III: A Blueprint for Action, guides the formulation of a strategic BI roadmap that provides business decision-makers with a clear, coherent implementation path that can be executed and managed within the constraints of the organization's available resources. It includes recommendations and provides advice on the critical success factors for BI implementations.

For SMEs to survive and compete globally with larger, more well-resourced organizations, business agility is an essential capability. SMEs have an opportunity to combine agility with their natural flexibility as a distinctive competitive advantage that typically eludes larger organizations confined by more formal structures and bureaucracy. Recent history is replete with evidence of smaller, more agile organizations that have leveraged business analytics to outcompete and overtake larger incumbents. This book will provide an essential tool in the arsenal of SME business and IT managers to enhance their chances of competing effectively and sustaining their existence in the Digital economy.

PART I

BI LANDSCAPE –
OPPORTUNITIES
FOR SMEs

Business Intelligence (BI) has become a strategic initiative for many organizations. Successful BI implementations have generated significant increases in revenue and cost savings. However, the failure rates are also very high. One of the reasons for these high failure rates is that the traditional BI methods are not suited to all organizations; they are seen by some as being too rigid and resource intensive. Additionally, the focus of the analytics is often at the localized level rather than on developing enterprise-wide analytical capabilities. Due to the resource intensity and rigidity of the traditional methods Small and Medium-Sized Enterprises (SMEs) have not embraced BI as an opportunity for them to compete with some of the larger players in their field using agility as their key advantage. Part I provides the context of the book by describing the BI landscape and identifying the opportunities that BI provides for SMEs especially as it relates to their ability to be more agile in their execution of BI.

Chapter 1 focuses on SMEs, what is unique about them and why there is a need to consider ICT adoption specifically for them. A general overview of SMEs is provided and then the particular barriers they face in terms of ICT adoption (e.g. lack of technology, expertise and knowledge) are discussed in more detail. Whatever the barriers, it must be recognized that there are also several opportunities for SMEs to use these technologies to their advantage and, by so doing, build a competitive advantage. However, these SMEs must recognize that traditional ICT technologies and methods may not be suited to their needs/characteristics. BI solutions are one such area where it has been felt that the technologies are just too costly and resource intensive for SMEs, and thus they have been slow to adopt them. This SME chapter provides the context for the discussions throughout the rest of the book as it relates to strategic BI specific to SMEs.

Chapter 2 describes a proposed methodology, an *Agile Integrated Methodology for Strategic Business Intelligence (AIMS-BI)*, which supports the agility and strategic perspective needed to achieve optimal business value from BI initiatives. Although this methodology can be applied to any organization looking at developing enterprise-wide analytic capabilities, it is particularly applicable to organizations that may not be suited to traditional BI methods due to limited resources and the need to demonstrate value quickly, such as SMEs.

AIMS-BI provides a systematic and structured approach that is enterprise-wide in reach yet agile in execution and focused on organizational needs and capabilities. The final output, a strategic BI roadmap, identifies the key BI opportunities, sets out a visible program of implementation and positions the organization to secure the executive commitment and resources required to maximize the BI business value.

1

Barriers and Strategies for Enterprise ICT Adoption in SMEs

A point of view can be a dangerous luxury when [used in place of] insight and understanding

Marshall McLuhan

Introduction (Digital Economy – Implications for Business)

For some time now, business analysts and practitioners have contemplated the onset of the Knowledge Economy in which economic growth and competitiveness become increasingly dependent on the capacity to create, process, accumulate and disseminate knowledge. This includes knowledge about customers, products, processes and competitors, or even knowledge itself as a competitive, tradable asset. Businesses that acquired knowledge by way of closed innovation processes or through the accumulation of knowledge assets (e.g. patents) were able to maintain sustained competitive differentiation.

The more recent emergence of the digital economy has accelerated the onset of the knowledge economy and changed its competitive dynamics by significantly lowering the cost of acquiring and processing of data, information and knowledge. This change has created opportunities for greater participation by organizations with less resources.

Among the disruptive digital technologies that are driving this evolution are the following:

Cloud Computing: It allows businesses to outsource their computing infrastructure and access high quality servers, network and application resources on demand and without the traditional attendant capital and operating costs or management responsibility. This provides a rapid deployment capability for new products and services and enhanced business agility.

Mobile Computing: The ubiquitous mobile phone provides an on-demand channel to customers and consumers in order to engage, inform, educate, analyze and source/deliver digital transactions. This enables businesses to embed mobility in the way they design and deliver products and services.

Big Data Analytics: Incredibly large volumes of data are being generated each day, hour, minute from a variety of sources, including mobile data, e-Commerce transactions, social media traffic, web clickstreams and the Internet of Things (IoT). Access, retrieval and analysis of these powerful real-time information flows at the point of creation is becoming more valuable than any legacy knowledge, and provides the basis for enhanced business intelligence.

Advances in Machine Learning and Artificial Intelligence: Provide enhanced algorithms that decrease information processing costs through the digitization and automation of knowledge work. Well-designed algorithms can provide businesses with sophisticated capabilities in areas such as marketing campaigns, credit risk management, logistics and e-Commerce recommender systems.

Social Media: Provides digital channels of engagement, information and interaction with customers and consumers. Businesses of all sizes can no longer afford to ignore social media which increasingly shapes and reflects public sentiment, opinions and consensus.

Companies that are slow to adopt these advanced digital ICTs as an integral part of their business operations and capabilities, or adapt to the increased competitive dynamics and complexity of the way modern business is being conducted in this evolving landscape, will find it difficult to survive. By extension, countries that fail to encourage and facilitate broad-based ICT adoption within the local business community will find it difficult to compete in the emerging digital economy.

SMEs and ICT in Developing Economies

While AIMS-BI is highly adaptable and designed to be broadly applicable to both small and large enterprises in developed and developing economies, the primary focus of this book is on SMEs in developing countries.

Micro, small and medium-sized enterprises (mSMEs) are considered to be one of the main forces in economic growth and job creation, not only in developed economies, but also in emerging economies or economies in transition.[1] Globally, close to 140 million SMEs in 130 countries account for 65% of the total labor force (Kotelnikov, 2007). Furthermore, the impact of SMEs in the domestic economy go well beyond employment and GDP to contribute substantially to the production and distribution of goods and services, and the enhancement of innovation, productivity and competitiveness (Witter and Kirton, 1990).

The drive for the increased adoption and use of ICTs in developing countries is theorized to be a catalyst that could help these countries leapfrog the stages of development undergone by more developed nations (Steinmueller, 2001). Given the importance of SMEs to the domestic economy of these countries, there is considerable interest in facilitating the progressive adoption and use of ICTs by SMEs. These ICTs can play a significant role in helping SMEs to improve their operating performance and business competitiveness, and hence their contribution to economic growth. Notwithstanding the obvious benefits and competitive imperative of adopting ICTs, SMEs are often overwhelmed and unsure about the path they need to take to realize the benefits that are being touted by experts, vendors and other companies in the global landscape and often miss the opportunity that these technologies can afford. As a result, the consistent adoption and effective diffusion of advanced ICT solutions among the small business sector in developing economies have continued to be elusive.

SMEs and ICT Adoption – Barriers & Challenges

A number of factors have been identified as barriers to ICT adoption by SMEs and they are based on the premise that the characteristics

---

[1] https://oecd.org/industry/smes/31919278.pdf.

of small firms are different from those of their larger counterparts. Similarly, the factors that affect the adoption and use of ICT in large organizations are not necessarily the same as those that affect SMEs. Consequently, theories that explain adoption in large organizations may not be applicable to small businesses. Small firms, in comparison to larger firms, require different managerial approaches since there are fundamental differences between the two. The low level of ICT literacy and awareness of SME owners and employees, the cost of acquiring technology, the lack of suitable financing options, the lack of the business analytic skills, data quality issues, the lack of skills to identify the business questions that need to be answered and the absorptive capacity to effectively deploy ICT-enabled solutions have all been identified as issues specific to SMEs. Generally, it is not a trivial decision for any organization to adopt ICT; there are numerous factors that need to be considered when the utilization of ICT is being contemplated. This is especially so in the case of SMEs as they often lack financial and human resources.

Several other factors, including the characteristics of the firm, the orientation of the CEO and the type of industry have been deemed to be influential in the ICT adoption decision of small businesses. Constraints on financial resources and the lack of in-house IT expertise increase the level of risk that an investment in IT will represent to smaller companies. Additionally, the individual characteristics of the CEOs as well as their attitudes to ICT and innovation and their level of ICT knowledge are strong determinants of adoption as they are the main decision-makers in the organization. SMEs led by CEOs with positive attitudes toward ICTs are more likely to adopt, particularly if they perceive that ICTs that are compatible with their operations and comparatively easy to use will be beneficial to their organization.

One important finding from empirical investigations into ICT adoption by SMEs, is that intermediaries play a crucial role in the adoption of complex applications by SMEs (Brown and Lockett, 2004). They also found that the aggregation of advanced ICT solutions, such as e-Business applications, to provide services to SMEs as a group rather than to individuals will encourage their adoption. These insights suggest that Cloud Computing and Software-as-a-Service (SaaS) which offer fully hosted ICT application solutions, could provide a feasible alternative for SMEs seeking sophisticated ICT services at relatively low costs, rather than having to purchase and manage these systems and services for themselves. Thompson and Brown (2008) further investigated the key roles that intermediaries perform in enabling the ICT adoption process by SMEs in developing countries. These roles include knowledge dissemination, financial partnership, technical advising and solution provision. The AIMS-BI methodology and the guidelines presented throughout this book fulfill key aspects of this facilitating role.

BI – Value Opportunities for SMEs

In our introductory chapter, we discuss our use of the term business intelligence (BI) to represent a wide range of data-driven decision support applications including data warehousing, data mining, business analytics, online analytic processing, performance management and knowledge management. Collectively, BI is generally considered to be a means of "combining data gathering, data storage, and knowledge management with analytical tools to present complex and competitive information to planners and decision makers" (Negash and Gray, 2008). Embracing the notion of "Data as an Asset" and establishing an explicit Data Governance mechanism to manage, secure and exploit the value of data have become key success factors for deriving strategic value from Information Technology.

The stories of globally successful startups, such as Netflix, increase awareness and provide motivation for SMEs to adopt BI, with many senior executives clearly recognizing the strategic opportunity that BI represents to their businesses. While such celebrated cases might be considered exceptional, the BI value opportunities for SMEs are nevertheless considerable. Typical examples include the following:

Distribution and Retail

> *Market basket analysis*: It increases understanding of customers' buying behaviors and identifies those items they tend to purchase together. This knowledge can improve stocking, store layout strategies and marketing promotions.

Sales forecasting: Examining time-based and location-based sales patterns helps retailers to understand buying seasonality in order to make optimal supply and stocking decisions.

Merchandise planning and allocation: When retailers contemplate new stores or market expansion, they can improve merchandise planning and allocation by examining patterns in stores or regions with similar demographic characteristics.

Distribution logistics: Distribution companies can use low-cost GPS data collectors with operational dashboards that enable managers to visualize route performance and facilitate decision-making in real time. Based on continual analysis of each driver's data, route optimization can save significant fuel costs and enhance delivery services for customers.

Credit and Micro-Finance Services

Credit Decision Analysis: Default and bad debt can be enormously costly in micro-finance operations and are among the factors that drives high lending rates. By analyzing past transactions that were known to be fraudulent or to default, operators can optimize and reduce the transaction costs of their credit decisions.

Predictive life-cycle value: Repeat clients are a common feature of micro-finance operations. Data mining can help operators to predict each customer's lifetime value and behavior patterns to service segments and individuals appropriately (e.g., time-based offers of special deals and discounts).

These are just a few examples of the kinds of data-driven analytics solutions that are no longer available exclusively to large scale enterprises but are now accessible to small and medium-sized companies.

The world of the artificial (man-made institutions, artifacts and their interactions) is not getting any smaller. The rate at which data is being generated from human social and commercial interactions is growing exponentially. Long before Big Data Analytics and Machine Learning Algorithms became fashionable business terms, Edward Wilson made this perennial assertion:

We are drowning in information, while starving for wisdom. The world henceforth will be run by synthesizers, people able to put together the right information at the right time, think critically about it, and make important choices wisely.

Wilson (1999)

Wilson's "synthesizers" forecast the ascendancy of today's Analytics Competitors, organizations such as Google, Amazon, Capital One and Netflix, that make widespread use of BI and Data Assets to create significant business value.

With currently available digital technology options, the capabilities of BI are much more accessible to SMEs than before and there is increased recognition and acceptance by SME leaders of the value opportunities that strategic BI creates. However, the availability of mechanisms to support such organizations in the implementation of BI at a strategic level are limited in literature and practice. In the Appendix we provide examples of the use of the AIMS-BI Methodology to enable various kinds of BI applications. The remainder of this book provides business and technology executives in SMEs with clear, step-by-step directions for applying AIMS-BI in the development of a customized BI roadmap to value-creation that is tailored to their own businesses.

2

AN AGILE INTEGRATED METHODOLOGY FOR STRATEGIC BUSINESS INTELLIGENCE (AIMS-BI)

Art and science have their meeting point in method.

Edward G. Bulwer-Lytto

Introduction

Organizations that aspire to become data-driven competitors by developing a data-driven decision-making culture need to develop an analytic orientation and BI capabilities *enterprise wide*. Within the strategy domain, BI is considered to be an enabler of organizational transformation that can be employed at the enterprise level to introduce new business models and business strategies, and fundamentally change the way a company competes in the marketplace. Therefore, "Business Intelligence (BI) has become a strategic initiative and is now recognized by chief information officers and business leaders as instrumental in driving business effectiveness and innovation".[1] This view is reinforced by a growing body of evidence pointing to the strategic benefits of BI. However, there are also high failure rates and cases where companies have spent more resources than their competitors on BI solutions with a smaller Return on Investment (ROI) and at the same time have seen their market share and customer base shrink. Many organizational BI initiatives struggle through a myriad of technology platforms, reporting tools and localized data sources that fail to deliver consistent information that can drive value-added and timely executive decision-making. These organizations may not

---

[1] http://gartner.com/newsroom/id/500680.

even recognize that it is their own organizational weaknesses (e.g. data security, data access, metadata management and data quality) that hinder their BI efforts.

Small and Medium-Sized Enterprises (SMEs), in particular, can be challenged by the technical complexity and resource requirements of traditional BI solutions. The need to provide agility and strategic level BI for such organizations is the motivation behind the design of this new methodology and is guided by the question: *What hybrid methodology will allow for a more nimble and agile approach to enterprise business intelligence, especially for those organizations with resource and expertise constraints?*

Organizations seeking to deploy agile yet enterprise-level BI need an effective means of assessing the current state and maturity of their enterprise information management (IM) practices and of identifying and addressing critical gaps that could inhibit the desired returns on successful BI investments. The focus of the analytics is often at the localized level rather than on developing enterprise-wide analytical capabilities. A methodology that can resolve the dichotomy between strategic enterprise-scale BI and the more agile, lower startup cost profile of BI initiatives focused in a specific functional area is important for SMEs with resource and expertise constraints.

Analytics Competitors have been described by Davenport and Harris (2007) as organizations that improve performance through the application of data analytics to their business processes. An important feature of these organizations is that they apply analytics in a structured way, as part of an organizational strategy, championed by top leadership and delivered through an integrated enterprise approach, to empower decision-makers at every level. A Gartner report emphasizes the need for structured frameworks that help business and IT leaders "architect a more complete plan for business intelligence (BI), analytics and performance management (PM) that will align people, processes and applications, and ultimately yield better returns".[2] A key insight from the report is that each organization needs to derive the appropriate configuration (e.g. roadmap) based on its own strategic objectives and business circumstances. The methodology outlined

---

[2] https://gartner.com/doc/1209327/gartners-business-intelligence-analytics-performance.

in this chapter provides a sequence of steps that will produce, as its ultimate output, this configuration.

Davenport and Harris (2007) describe many exemplars of organizations that, by employing an enterprise approach with strong senior management advocacy and leadership, make widespread use of Business Analytics and Data Assets to create significant value for their business. They suggest a path that organizations need to traverse in order to arrive at a state of being an "Analytics Competitor" in which the organization consistently realizes a stream of rich insights from BI that it is able to translate into actionable value. This path typically requires navigating through a critical stage (stage 2) in which functional analytics initiatives are used to build momentum and secure executive interest. The next stage, stage 3, requires an executive commitment and resource allocation to a strategic BI vision. While the functional analytical initiatives are supported by a number of existing knowledge discovery process models, methodologies for moving from functional to enterprise-wide BI are lacking, thereby preventing organizations from reaching stage 3. AIMS-BI fills this void.

This chapter describes a methodology that addresses the need for implementing strategic *yet* agile BI in organizations; an *AIMS-BI*. The methodology supports the agility and strategic perspective needed to achieve optimal business value from BI initiatives. It will enable organizations to derive appropriate configurations (i.e. a BI roadmap) based on its own strategic objectives and business circumstances. AIMS-BI integrates a number of existing techniques, including information maturity assessment, multi-criteria decision-making and proof of concepts through prototyping, to support the agility and strategic perspective needed to achieve optimal business value from BI initiatives. The methodology is a multiphase solution that helps the organization understand not just *what* needs to be done but also *when*, *how* and *why*. Thus, it describes the activities, methods, tools and techniques that should be used throughout the process.

Why the Need for New Methodologies?

The Need for a Strategic, yet Agile Perspective

The value of adopting a defined systematic and repeatable process in planning and carrying out data-driven initiatives has been widely accepted. There are a number of existing process models which, collectively, have been termed Knowledge Discovery and Data Mining (KDDM) process models. Currently the most commonly used of these is the CRoss-Industry Standard Process for data mining (CRISP-DM) which consists of six steps: (1) Business Understanding; (2) Data Understanding; (3) Data Preparation; (4) Modeling; (5) Evaluation; and (6) Deployment. These models assume that the organization is in a ready position to adopt BI tools and techniques. However, in reality this may not be the case and if significant investments are made in the BI tools and techniques without the prerequisite factors in place, the BI initiatives will fail. AIMS-BI provides a methodology for assessing this state of readiness, identifying the capability gaps and developing a strategic path forward in a very agile way.

Previously, there were two main approaches to BI that are often viewed as dichotomous – Strategic vs Tactical. The strategic approach is the top-down, integrated enterprise approach prescribed by both Davenport and Harris (2007) and Gartner's Business Intelligence and Performance Management Framework,[3] and is consistent with the "Bill Inmon" view of the Corporate DW (Inmon, 2005) as the *"single organizational repository of enterprise wide data across many lines of business and subject areas that: Contains massive and integrated data; Represents the complete organizational view of information needed to run and understand the business"*. The alternative contending tactical approach derives from the contemporary view of Ralph Kimball, who prescribes a bottom-up, dimensional approach to BI based on functional data marts which are ultimately aggregated into the corporate DW. The Inmon vs Kimball debate is well represented in the literature. Breslin (2004) summarizes the essential differences between both approaches (see Table 2.1).

The Kimball approach allows for a more agile, lower start-up costs and quicker delivery of a BI solution that is tactical and focused in a specific functional area of the business. However, critics are of the view that this approach tends to lack integration between disparate initiatives and enterprise scalability, and, due to its lack of a strategic focus, is unlikely to achieve transformational data-driven impacts.

---

[3] http://umsl.edu/~sauterv/DSS4BI/links/pdf/BI/gartners_business_intelligen_142827.pdf.

Table 2.1   Characteristics Favoring Inmon's or Kimball's Model

CHARACTERISTIC	FAVORS KIMBALL	FAVORS INMON
Nature of the organization's decision support requirements	Tactical	Strategic
Data integration requirements	Individual business areas	Enterprise-wide integration
Structure of data	Business metrics, performance measures and scorecards	Non-metric data and for data that will be applied to meet multiple and varied information needs
Scalability	Need to adapt to highly volatile needs within a limited scope	Growing scope and changing requirements are critical
Persistency of data	Source systems are relatively stable	High rate of change from source systems
Staffing and skills requirements	Small teams of generalists	Larger team(s) of specialists
Time to delivery	Need for the first data warehouse application is urgent	Organization's requirements allow for longer start-up time
Cost to deploy	Lower start-up costs, with each subsequent project costing about the same	Higher start-up costs, with lower subsequent project development costs

On the other hand, the Inmon approach is strategic in nature, and architected for enterprise integration, but demands higher start-up costs and longer delivery times, can be rigid and may be difficult for some organizations to undertake, especially those constrained by the requisite skills, resources and time requirements of this approach. AIMS-BI can bridge the gap between the two approaches as it supports organizations in becoming analytical aspirants using a strategic yet agile approach.

Know the Current State of your Information Maturity

The previous approaches to BI, whether tactical or strategic, consider the adoption of BI techniques and technologies without necessarily ensuring that the organization is in a state of readiness for BI. One important aspect that needs to be considered is the state of its IM maturity. A number of models are available for assessing different aspects of maturity within the organization but for AIMS-BI we have adapted an IM maturity model which is used by organizations to assess their current state in terms of the maturity of their IM practices and to identify gaps in these areas. These IM maturity models provide organizations with a formal means of identifying capability gaps in enterprise IM disciplines, critical for strategic BI success. Performing these periodic maturity assessments can help organizations to monitor and measure how improvements have helped to close the identified gaps.

End User and Key Stakeholder Engagement

A key component of ensuring the agility of the methodology is the engagement of the end users and key stakeholders early in the process and their inclusion in key decision-making related to the BI initiatives that should be pursued. This inclusionary approach is important as the stakeholders must feel that they are a part of key decision-making. Since the decision about the choice of BI initiatives is subjective, with different groups having contending views, group subjective decision techniques become very useful in this process. Therefore the Analytical Hierarchical Processing (AHP) technique was integrated into AIMS-BI.

Design of AIMS-BI

AIMS-BI was developed using the Design Science research methodology which provides a set of guidelines for the development and evaluation of ICT artifacts to address real-world problems. AIMS-BI is the artifact that has been developed to provide organizations, such as SMEs, with a prescriptive methodology for guiding the organization on a path to strategic BI.

Design science research requires the rigorous evaluation of the artifact using one of a number of proposed evaluation techniques. AIMS-BI has been evaluated using primary cases studies; where its application in the business environment was analyzed in depth.

AIMS-BI starts with an assessment of the organization's information maturity (Step 1) and progresses to the development of BI prototypes (Step 4). This methodology bridges the gap between knowing and doing. The early stages emphasize "knowing" about the organization, identifying strategic priorities and discovering BI

Table 2.2 Relevant Techniques

#	STEP OF AIMS-BI	EXISTING TECHNIQUES USED	KEY OUTPUTS/OUTCOMES
1	Information maturity assessment	Survey design & administration; capability assessment	IM assessment report; information maturity capability baseline; gap analysis
2	BI opportunity discovery	Semi-structured interviews; case study analysis	Business understanding, strategic priorities; discovery of BI opportunities; portfolio of Proof-of-Concept (PoC) initiatives
3	BI portfolio evaluation	Stakeholder engagement/priority assessment; PoC value assessment/strategic alignment; Multi-Criteria Decision Making (MCDM) a	Select priority PoC initiatives; key executive/participant awareness & engagement
4	Proof of concept prototypes	Technology deployment; agile software prototype development; Knowledge Discovery/Data Mining (KDDM); data profiling/quality assessment	Data integration/data as a service technology sandbox; proof-of-concept analytics prototypes; systematic process for data quality management/metrics; valuation of data assets
5	Strategic BI roadmap	BI portfolio planning & strategic alignment	Strategic BI roadmap

opportunities. The latter stages focus on the "doing" aspect of BI, including experimentation and the demonstration of business value, and culminate with the strategic BI roadmap which provides the organization with a pathway for strategic BI.

To ensure the rigor of the development of AIMS-BI, existing literature was analyzed to identify relevant methods and/or techniques that should be integrated into the methodology. These methods and techniques, which include capability assessment surveys, interviews, technology deployments, multi-criteria decision-making techniques, KDDM, modeling and data analytics, are summarized in Table 2.2.

Description of AIMS-BI

The adoption of the readily accessible BI tools, technologies and data assets alone is not enough to give organizations the distinctive competitive advantage they are looking for through BI. Rather it is the complex organizational systems and structures, processes, employee expertise and executive commitment in combination with these tools, technologies and data assets that provide this advantage. Therefore, organizations seeking to effectively deploy strategic BI need an effective means of assessing the current state and maturity of their enterprise IM practices and identifying critical gaps that could present barriers and inhibit the desired returns on BI investments.

Furthermore, there is a need for methodologies that can resolve the dichotomy between strategic enterprise-scale BI and the more agile, lower startup cost profile of BI initiatives focused in a specific functional area of the business. This ability is especially important for those organizations, such as SMEs, that have shied away from investing in strategic BI solutions due to the perceived high cost and intensive resource requirements often associated with these strategic solutions. Therefore, the AIMS-BI methodology proposed is *enterprise in scope* yet *agile in execution* and considers, not just the BI tools and technologies and data assets, but also other factors of importance to BI at the strategic level. The final output of this methodology – the strategic BI roadmap - consists of a dynamic portfolio of initiatives that are strategic in nature yet modular, thus allowing for agile execution.

The relevant techniques described in Table 2.2 were synthesized into a repeatable methodology referred to as an "Agile Methodology for Strategic Business Intelligence – AIMS-BI" (Figure 2.1) which consists of four steps culminating in the generation of a comprehensive strategic BI roadmap. One of the aims of this methodology is to guide organizations in knowing not just what needs to be done, but also how it can be done. Each of the steps is described below.

Step 1: Information Maturity Assessment

The key foundational step of AIMS-BI is the IM maturity assessment that will enable the organization to assess and benchmark their Enterprise IM capabilities. This provides the setting within which BI initiatives are conceptualized, developed and deployed in order to deliver the maximum strategic benefits to the organization. The IM assessment recognizes that enterprise-level BI capabilities are complex, hierarchical and multifaceted in nature, comprising not only information resources and data assets, but also organizational structures, people skills and processes. The results of this assessment provide the organization with a good understanding of its baseline BI

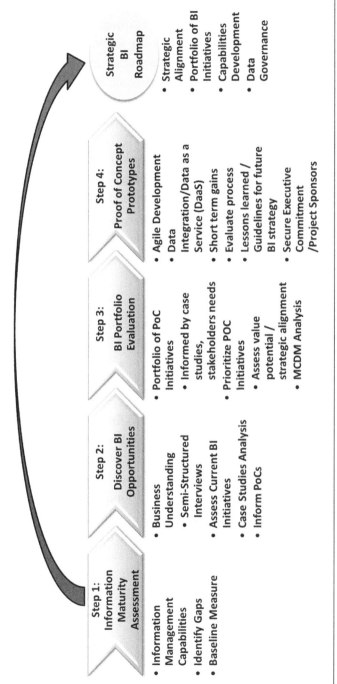

Figure 2.1   AIMS-BI.

readiness and identify areas of weaknesses that must be addressed if it is to compete on analytics. Periodic IM maturity assessments, conducted through self- or third-party assessment, and benchmarking, help to establish an informed basis for formulating effective IM development programs and tracking continuous improvement.

The outputs of this step form an important input to the BI roadmap as they identify key areas that the organization should focus on improving if they are to achieve the benefits of strategic BI. This IM assessment provides a number of benefits: (i) It allows the organization to quickly determine the state of its IM capabilities as a precursor to formulating an enterprise-wide analytics strategy; (ii) It is done by the stakeholders which ensures stakeholder/user participation early in the process; (iii) It does not require a significant investment of expertise or financial resources so is suited to SMEs.

The IM assessment process is described in more depth in Chapter 3.

Step 2: BI Opportunity Discovery

This step is concerned with arriving at a thorough understanding of stakeholders and their business needs and identifying strategic BI opportunities for the organization. This is achieved by using semi-structured interviews to better understand the business processes, to assess any current BI initiatives that the organization has in place or is considering, and discovering BI opportunities. Many organizations have some idea of the areas which they think would benefit from the application of BI (e.g. Customer and Product Analytics) and these are explored further. In parallel with gaining an understanding what already exists within the given organization, an understanding of what similar organizations have achieved though BI initiatives and their critical success factors, is obtained through a review of case studies. This allows the organization to be clear, not just about what they are thinking of investing in, but, importantly, identify areas in which others, globally, have had strategic BI success.

This step may also include other useful opportunity discovery activities such as:

   i. A BI introspection session – a facilitated session, that should involve the executive leadership and management team, in which the organization's vision and aspirations and the opportunities and barriers to becoming a BI competitor are examined.

ii. An Opportunity Discovery Workshop – a facilitated workshop with key operations and management team members in which the IM assessment findings from Step 1 are shared and opportunities for BI initiatives and organizational priorities are "discovered" through key stakeholder engagement. This active involvement of key stakeholders is one of the critical success factors for BI projects.

The BI opportunities that are identified from this step form the basis for the development of a portfolio of BI initiatives.

Step 3: BI Portfolio Evaluation

The aim of this step is to develop and prioritize a set of Proof of Concepts (PoCs) from the portfolio of possible BI initiatives. It is unlikely that organizations, especially SMEs, will have the expertise, skills and other resources to tackle all the possible BI opportunities. Executives and key decision-makers will have their own preferences for which BI initiatives are to be implemented; however, there are a number of criteria to consider in this prioritization process. Therefore a subjective, multi-criteria, group decision-making technique can be used to make the process unbiased yet participatory. One such technique is Analytical Hierarchical Processing (AHP) which provides a framework for solving different types of multi-criterion decision problems based on the relative priorities assigned to each criterion's role in achieving the stated objective.

In order to more accurately estimate the potential value to the organization of each initiative, further information is elicited from the stakeholders through online forms and semi-structured interviews. A combination of these and other inputs, including the results from the IM Assessment (from Step 1), are used to define a set of possible PoCs tailored to the organization's context and strategic priorities which can be used to demonstrate the value of BI to key stakeholders for organizational buy-in. Further details about the BI opportunity discovery and portfolio evaluation steps are provided in Chapter 4.

Step 4: Proof of Concept Prototypes

The top PoCs to be developed into prototypes, with the available resources, are selected from the portfolio of prioritized initiatives. The ability to rapidly mobilize BI prototypes requires a flexible platform in order to connect to heterogeneous, non-conventional internal and external sources of data to evaluate and better control the scope, cost and timeline of their implementation. The traditional Extract, Transform and Load (ETL)/Data Warehousing applications for Data Integration are considered to be too rigid and resource and time intensive to support the agility being sought in AIMS-BI generally and, more specifically, for the development of the prototypes. However, the emerging disciplines of *Data Virtualization* and *Data as a Service* present alternative approaches to the traditional ETL/Data Warehousing applications for Data Integration and provide a range of functions and Data Delivery Services that enable Agile BI. Furthermore there are a number of Open Source solutions for these services which allow for the rapid development of the prototypes without significant investments in tools and technologies. The use of open-source Data Integration software provides for a level of deployment agility and experimentation that yields significant reductions in lead-time, cost and time-to-value, and will ultimately help to inform the BI investment decisions.

The prototypes, by demonstrating the strategic value of BI, allow the members of the executive team to better understand the potential of these investments. In turn, this will help to get the "buy-in" from senior management that is so critical to the success of strategic BI. The development of the prototypes can also help in the early identification of problems that may have to be addressed before investing significant resources in a full-blown BI strategy. They provide the organization with a good sense of how much time and resources will have to be invested in order to get the data to a form that is suited for the analytics required. The use of Open Source data integration software to support the prototypes provides a level of deployment agility and experimentation that yields significant reductions in lead-time, cost and time-to-value. Additionally, given that the prototypes are deployed using iterative, prototyping techniques that allow for active user engagement and experimentation, they support agility.

The details of the development of PoC prototypes are provided in Chapter 5.

Strategic Business Intelligence Roadmap

The final output of AIMS-BI is the strategic BI roadmap which provides the organization with a balanced portfolio of BI initiatives and a pathway for establishing a strategic BI capability. Both the maturity assessment and the PoCs are integral to the development of the BI roadmap as they identify key areas on which the organization needs to focus and develop capabilities if it is to maximize the benefits of its investment in strategic BI. The roadmap will typically include technology and applications projects as well as capacity building/training, governance structures/roles and policy initiatives – all critical factors that are required to be in place to support the implementation of these initiatives.

The roadmap is designed in such a way that, even though it is Enterprise-wide in scope, the organization can plan its execution incrementally, based on its own absorptive capacity for change, without overcommitting financial or human resources. The completed prototypes provide key bootstrap initiatives that can lead to important early success and demonstrable value in the execution of the roadmap. The mixture of developmental and applied initiatives will allow the critical gaps identified from the IM Assessment to be addressed, while concurrently generating early returns from delivering new BI capabilities.

By highlighting key decisions, integration points, gaps and dependencies, the roadmap is amenable to formal program management execution to balance resources and investments across the multiple BI, analytics and infrastructure initiatives and projects. The built-in annual IM maturity assessment provides a systematic means by which the organization can measure improvements in its IM and BI capabilities and will help executives track the realized business impact and effectiveness of the BI program as it is rolled out.

Further details for the development of the strategic BI roadmap are provided in Chapter 8.

Findings from Applying AIMS-BI

AIMS-BI was evaluated using the case studies of both a financial organization and an academic institution. Both organizations were grappling with the issue of how to get more value from their data and were in the early stages of investing in BI. Both, therefore, were open to allowing AIMS-BI to be applied to their organizations.

After the application of the methodology in these organizations, key stakeholders were interviewed to ascertain the value they saw in applying the methodology. Some of the findings were:

1. The stakeholders felt that the IM assessment proved to be extremely useful in identifying the state of readiness of the organization for strategic BI. It helped them to identify a number of areas that would have to be addressed in order to maximize the benefits of its BI investment. Further, the findings from the PoC prototypes supported the findings of the maturity assessment. For example, in both case studies, the assessment identified issues with data quality and, in developing the PoC, specific issues of data quality were identified (e.g. the inconsistency in data values generally and, more specifically and concerning, in those fields used to join tables). The interviewees felt the IM assessment was an extremely valuable first step. The results of the assessment process provided empirical evidence in support of their perceived weaknesses and shortcomings. This provides a stronger case for investing resources to address these weaknesses. They were also of the view that the assessment should not be administered solely by the internal team but rather in the partnered approach (i.e. include an independent third-party) as it was felt that a purely internal approach could be perceived as biased.

2. There was also affirmation for the inclusion of the key stakeholders and decision-makers in the development and evaluation of the BI portfolio. It was felt that their inclusion, especially in the form of a workshop, allowed these diverse groups to weigh the options in terms of what should be prioritized and why in a collaborative way. The view was that the stakeholders might have felt excluded if they were not a part of the process and their buy-in is important.

3. The PoCs and, more specifically, the development of the prototypes demonstrated to the executive management team and
all key stakeholders the business value of BI, the systematic
approaches to better data quality management, the importance of data governance and the agility of data as a service
(DaaS). This secured/reinforced executive commitment to the
process. In fact, one of the organizations felt that even closer
collaboration and engagement would have been beneficial for
further transfer of knowledge from the external team to the
data analysts etc.

The findings from the case study also support the literature in terms
of some of the critical success factors, these included:

1. The need for a champion within the organization. The financial organization's project manager turned out to be this
champion and the success of the study can be attributed, in
large part, to this person as she ensured that the sponsors and
executive team were available to meet with the researchers in
a timely manner.
2. Data quality is critical to BI success. In both case studies, data
quality received a low score from the IM assessment and the
development of a formal data quality process was included as
an early, mandatory initiative in both the BI roadmaps.

Conclusion

It is being recognized that the traditional methods for BI are too complex and rigid, costly, time consuming and resource intensive for many
organizations and there is, thus, a need for lower cost, less resource
intensive, agile approaches to strategic BI. AIMS-BI provides an agile
methodology for strategic BI. The method integrates various existing
techniques to generate a strategic BI roadmap that reflects the key BI
opportunities, a visible program of implementation, and secures the
executive commitment and resources required to put the organization
on the path to becoming a serious "Analytics Competitor".

The first step of AIMS-BI, IM assessment is critical as it identifies
a number of key areas in which the organization score may be low but
that are essential for BI success (e.g. data quality). Without addressing

the issues in these areas, the business value that could be achieved through BI investments would not be realized and senior management would consider the project a failure. The second step provided valuable insight into the current practices and opportunities within the organization. In the third step, the use of the subjective group decision-making technique is extremely useful as it engages senior management and ensures their commitment to the BI initiatives. The final output, a strategic BI Roadmap, identifies the key BI opportunities, sets out a visible program of implementation, and positions the organization to secure the executive commitment and resources required to maximize the BI business value. AIMS-BI provides a systematic and structured approach that is enterprise-wide in reach yet agile in execution and focused on organizational needs and capabilities. Although the primary output of AIMS-BI is the strategic BI roadmap, an important output of Step 4 would be the working prototypes that are at an advanced stage of development and will not require a great deal more effort for full deployment. AIMS-BI is enterprise in scope yet agile in execution and, if followed, can ensure that an organization maximizes its investments in strategic BI.

Although this methodology can be applied in any organization looking at developing enterprise-wide analytic capabilities, it is particularly applicable to organizations that may not be suited to traditional BI methods due to limited resources and the need to demonstrate value quickly, such as SMEs.

PART II

Navigating the Agile BI Process

This section describes the steps of the AIMS-BI methodology which details not just *what* should be done but also *how*. Thus, if followed carefully, these steps will navigate the organization to a position of being an analytics competitor. Each chapter highlights the importance of agility throughout the methodology and identifies ways in which this can be achieved. Recommendations for less resource-intensive options are also provided where possible. All these considerations will allow SMEs to be an important target group for AIMS-BI.

Chapter 3 describes the first key foundational step of AIMS-BI, the Information Management (IM) maturity assessment, which enables organizations to assess and benchmark their Enterprise IM capabilities as a precursor to formulating an Agile Business Intelligence (BI) strategy. The proposed IM maturity assessment model was developed by adapting, synthesizing and extending existing maturity models and methods. The IM maturity assessment enables the agile assessment of the IM capabilities at the enterprise level and across multiple domains including People/Organization, Policy, Technology, Compliance, Measurement and Process/Practice. Importantly, this key step responds to one of the oft-cited criticisms of Information Systems maturity models that is, although the primary purpose of maturity models is to assess and identify capability gaps, many models do not describe how to effectively perform the actions required to address the gaps identified. AIMS-BI addresses this "knowing-doing" gap by embedding the IM maturity assessment as the key foundational stage of the overall agile methodology.

Chapter 4 goes on to describe the next step of AIMS-BI – discovering BI opportunities. Based on the premise that it is unlikely that organizations, especially SMEs, have the resources to address all BI opportunities at once, this step provides guidance on how to build and evaluate a portfolio of BI initiatives in order to identify those that are perceived as likely to provide the greatest strategic value to the organization. Depending on the resources available and the resources needed for each, the top initiatives can be selected for implementation as Proof of Concepts (PoCs). This chapter highlights the opportunities for the engagement of key stakeholders in building this portfolio of initiatives which improves the agility of the methodology.

Chapter 5 describes the process models that can be used to build the analytics PoCs prototypes, for both Visualization and Data Mining. These process models are important as they provide a structured, systematic and repeatable process for analysts to follow to ensure the success of data-driven initiatives. Too many organizations, by taking an ad hoc approach to BI initiatives, are undermining the value that they can provide.

Chapter 6 describes some of the critical issues related to Data Quality (DQ) and Data Governance, which have been identified as two factors that constrain the efficiency and effectiveness of data-driven analytics initiatives and decision-making processes. The IM maturity assessment evaluates both DQ and Governance and provides details about particular issues that are affecting their overall scores. This chapter outlines what both DQ and Data Governance entail, explains why they are critical to BI and then goes on to describe, in detail, a systematic approach to DQ standards definitions and data quality measurement. The chapter will also demonstrate the use of DQ Dashboards in empowering data stewards to formulate and oversee adherence to DQ standards and policies across the organization. Throughout the emphasis will be on the systemic approaches to measurement, ranking and quantification of DQ and asset value and how these can be maintained through proper Data Governance practices.

Finally, Chapter 7 describes data integration which provides the decision-makers with the flexibility to explore on-demand, and prototype various BI initiatives. Business analysts and decision-makers require access to data sources in a timely manner, to experiment, prototype and evaluate various analytics initiatives. Achieving this timely access to data requires greater *agility* in data integration and the capability and tools to rapidly access and integrate data from multiple heterogeneous sources. This chapter describes the options for achieving this data integration and provides a detailed discussion of how agility can be achieved.

3

INFORMATION MANAGEMENT (IM) MATURITY ASSESSMENT

Evaluating Business Capabilities and Gaps

Without proper self-evaluation, failure is inevitable.

John Wooden

Introduction

There is a high failure rate for Business Intelligence (BI) initiatives and many organizations struggle through a myriad of technology platforms, reporting tools and localized data sources that not only fail to deliver value-added support for timely executive and management decision-making, but also expose the business to vulnerabilities in terms of data security, data access, data quality and data scalability issues (Jourdan et al., 2008).

One of the contributing factors to the high failure rate of BI initiatives is that many organizations launch initiatives without a clear sense of the state of the IM infrastructure, organizational capabilities, proper data quality and key business value opportunities. As organizations seek to exploit the potential of strategic BI, there is need for an effective means of assessing the current state and maturity of their Enterprise Information Management resources and practices and to identify critical gaps that could present barriers and inhibit the desired returns on, and success of, BI investments. It is important that this mechanism provides a high-level assessment perspective for executive management, while being granular enough to inform a systematic program of BI initiatives.

Information Management (IM) Maturity Assessment is a key foundational step in the proposed Agile Integrated Methodology for Strategic Business Intelligence (AIMS-BI) methodology as it enables organizations to assess and benchmark their Enterprise IM capabilities across multiple domains (i.e. People/Organization, Policy, Technology, Compliance, Measurement and Process/Practice) as a precursor to formulating an Agile Business Intelligence (BI) strategy. It provides the organization with some measures of its IM maturity across a number of domains and these measures can then be used to identify gaps and provide some baseline values for measuring improvements in IM capabilities when remedies are put into place. The results of the assessment provide the organization with a better understanding of their BI readiness. Maturity models, have increasingly been used by organizations as a systematic way to assess, measure and benchmark their capabilities in various domains. Examples include the Organizational Project Management Maturity Model (OPM3)[1] and the Capability Maturity Model Integration (CMMI).[2]

This chapter describes a proposed IM Maturity Model that was implemented as a component of AIMS-BI to enable organizations to assess and benchmark their Enterprise IM capabilities. The proposed model was developed by adapting, synthesizing and extending existing maturity models and methods and was used to develop an online survey instrument which organizations can adopt for carrying out their IM assessment. The model determines the organizational context within which BI initiatives should be conceptualized, developed and deployed, in order to deliver the maximum strategic benefits to the organization.

Importantly this key step responds to one of the oft-cited criticisms of Information Systems maturity models, i.e. although the primary purpose of maturity models is to assess and identify capability gaps, many models do not describe how to effectively perform the actions required to address the gaps identified. AIMS-BI addresses this "knowing-doing" gap by embedding the Information Maturity Assessment as the key foundational stage of the overall agile methodology.

---

[1] https://learning.oreilly.com/library/view/organizational-project-management/9781628250305/.

[2] https://cio.com/article/2437864/developer/process-improvement-capability-maturity-model-integration-cmmi-definition-and-solutions.html.

Maturity Models in Organizations

Maturity models have gained prominence as they allow organizations to assess, measure and benchmark organizational capabilities relating to Processes, Objects and People (Mettler, 2009). By identifying capability gaps through a formal assessment of *"Where am I today?"* vs *"Where would I like to be?"* organizations are able to determine their maturity (i.e. competency, capability, level of sophistication) within a selected domain and establish a systematic basis for an informed program of development and continuous improvement. Maturity models have been developed for specific domains such as software development, project management, business process management and IT business value. Perhaps the best known is the Capability Maturity Model Integration (CMMI), used to manage the software development processes, which integrates several derivative models from the very popular Capability Maturity Model (CMM).

Maturity models can generally be categorized as one of two types, Staged and Continuous: (i) *Staged or* Fixed-level maturity models distinguish a fixed number, typically five, of generic maturity levels. Each maturity level is associated with a number of focus areas (process areas in CMM) that have to be implemented satisfactorily or be in compliance with all specified requirements of one maturity level, before the organization can progress to the next level. The original CMM for software and its successors are typical of a staged model; (ii) *Continuous* or Focus-area maturity models, on the other hand, put emphasis on a number of focus areas or dimensions that have to be developed to achieve maturity in the target functional domain. This type of maturity model identifies capability levels within each focus area, thus allowing organizations to develop their capabilities or competencies within those focus areas without being restricted to the generic maturity levels. The overall maturity of the organization is then expressed as a combination of the specific maturity levels within the individual focus areas. The derivative CMMI allows for both staged and continuous representation.

Focus-area maturity models provide the flexibility to express granular interdependencies within and between the focus areas thus allowing organizations to define a balanced, incremental development path, taking all focus areas into account. This focus area approach becomes an important design consideration for BI maturity models, given the complex, hierarchical and multi-order nature of strategic BI capabilities.

Implementing the IM Maturity Model

The IM maturity model to support AIMS-BI was synthesized from a number of existing maturity models, developed for Enterprise Information Management/BI, based on the following criteria:

- The scope of the maturity model should cover the organization's Enterprise Information Management resources and practices as the context for deploying an agile BI capability.
- It should target both business and technology management and practitioners.
- It should be based on practitioner-oriented maturity models that have been validated by industry and practitioner application.
- The model should be multidimensional addressing the maturity of process (e.g. the maturity of data governance), people (e.g. level of analytical skills of business analysts) and artifacts (e.g. quality of data assets).
- The application of the maturity model should be based on an assessment tool that can be self- or third-party-administered to a combination of management and staff respondents.

Based on these criteria and a review of twelve BI Maturity Models, the AIMS-BI maturity model was synthesized from a combination of the MIKE2.0 IM QuickScan tool (Methodology for an Integrated Knowledge Environment)[3] and the IBM-DGC Maturity Model[4] (DGCMM). The MIKE2.0 IM QuickScan tool provides coverage of all three elements of people, process and object, while also providing detailed, granular coverage of twenty eight functional areas and contains a comprehensive set of Capability assessment questions that can be adapted and reused for different organizational contexts. Three new functional areas, Value Creation, Strategic Alignment and Data Usage Quality, along with additional questions to assess their capability were included in the synthesized model.

---

[3] www.openmethodology.org.

[4] https://935.ibm.com/services/uk/cio/pdf/leverage_wp_data_gov_council_maturity_model.pdf.

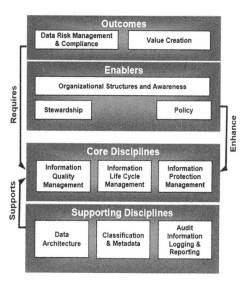

Figure 3.1 IBM data governance council maturity model.

The IBM-DGC Maturity Model (DGCMM) reflects close agreement and concurrence with the domains and functional areas in the MIKE2.0 IM Maturity Model. However, the DGCMM also provides the added benefit of emphasizing the interconnectedness and path dependencies between the various elements (see Figure 3.1). This is an important feature of *Continuous* or Focus-area maturity models as it allows for the crafting of a balanced, incremental development program, taking all focus areas into account (van Steenbergen et al., 2010).

The synthesized AIMS-BI IM maturity model examines information maturity on six dimensions: People/Organization, Policy, Technology, Compliance, Measurement and Process/Practice as follows:

1. People/Organization considers the human side of Information Management, how people are measured, motivated and supported in related activities. Organizations that motivate staff to think about information as a strategic asset tend to extract more value from their systems and overcome shortcomings in other categories.

2. Policy considers the message to staff from leadership and whether staff is required to administer and maintain information assets appropriately with consequences for inappropriate

behaviors. Without good policies and executive support, it is difficult to promote good practices even with the right supporting tools.

3. Technology assesses the tools that are provided to support IM activities. While technology on its own cannot fill gaps in the information resources, a lack of technological support makes it difficult to establish good practices. Given the technical nature of the content, only the IT representatives were required to answer these questions.

4. Compliance surveys the external IM obligations of the organization and helps assess how well an organization is prepared to meet targets from industry and external regulators. A low compliance score indicates that the organization is relying on luck rather than good practice to avoid regulatory and legal issues.

5. Measurement looks at how the organization identifies information issues and analyzes its data. Without measurement, it is impossible to sustainably manage the other aspects of the framework.

6. Process/Practice considers whether the organization has adopted standardized approaches to IM. Even with the right tools, measurement approaches, and policies, information assets cannot be sustained unless processes are consistently implemented. Poor processes result in inconsistent data and a lack of trust on the part of stakeholders.

For example, the assessment of the maturity of data stewardship in organizations will be measured at the level of supporting policy guidelines, technical infrastructure, process capability and measurement practice. The instrument is supported by an extensive set of capability statements that allows for a very granular assessment of organizational capabilities, the identification of gaps and the design of incremental programs of improvement.

The dimensional structures and functional areas evaluated by the synthesized maturity model are shown in Figure 3.2. The two questionnaire items shown illustrate how the policy and people dimension of data usage quality are assessed.

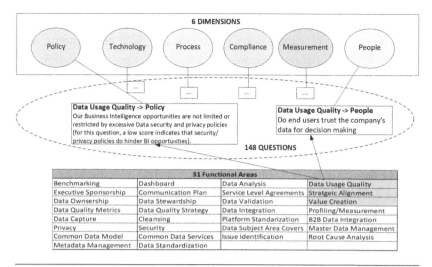

Figure 3.2 AIMS-BI synthesized IM maturity model.

Applying the AIMS-BI IM Maturity Assessment

A number of resources are available to support the AIMS-BI IM maturity assessment. These include an on-line survey instrument, integrated with a spreadsheet-based analysis and reporting tools, that is readily adaptable to different organizations. The questionnaire is typically administered in parallel with semi-structured interview sessions with various stakeholders and from these a final IM assessment report is generated.

Example of the Application of IM Maturity Assessment

Using a contrived case of an educational institution for illustrative purposes, the following example demonstrates how the AIMS-BI maturity assessment tool would be applied.

The IM Assessment is typically performed in parallel with semi-structured interview sessions and focus group workshops with a diverse set of stakeholders. The persons selected to participate in the IM assessment should constitute a representative cross-section of key business stakeholders. The IM maturity assessment is conducted using the AIMS-BI IM Maturity tool administered using the online instrument. The following narrative describes the typical output of such an assessment.

Figure 3.3 below shows the overall capability levels derived across the six high-level dimensions, through the IM assessment. The weighted result of this assessment is 1.6 out of a maximum of 5; the highest scores being assessed for Technology (2.0) and the lowest for Policy and Measurement (1.3).

Using the five levels of maturity for an organization, based on their IM practices, as proposed by META Group (see Table 3.1), the overall score of 1.6 would be categorized as reactive – meaning that there is minimal formalized Enterprise Information Management practices, except in isolated silos, and the organization reacts to data quality issues as they arise. More significantly, the higher levels of maturity in the Technology and Compliance categories suggest the existence of relatively sound traditional technology competencies and capabilities. However, the lower maturity scores for Policy and Measurement signal clear gaps in formal Data/Information Governance mechanisms and the minimal use of best practice behaviors and techniques such as data quality metrics and profiling/measurement. The overall need for improved Data Governance practices in areas such as Data quality management, ownership and stewardship is also manifest in the qualitative comments recorded from the various user group interviews.

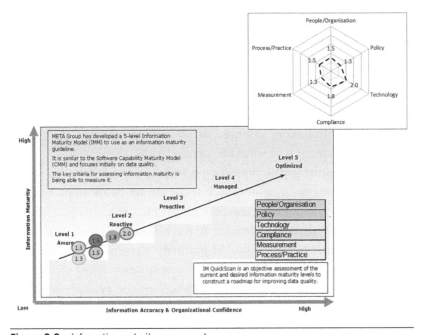

Figure 3.3 Information maturity assessment.

Table 3.1   Information Maturity Model (IMM) Capability Definitions

INFORMATION MATURITY MODEL CAPABILITY DEFINITIONS	
Level 1 – **Aware**	No common information practices. Any pockets of information management (IM) maturity that the organization has are based on the experience and initiatives of individuals
Level 2 – **Reactive**	Little in the way of Enterprise Information Management practices. However, certain departments are aware of the importance of professionally managing information assets and have developed common practices used within their projects. At the enterprise level, a level 2 organization reacts to data quality issues as they arise
Level 3 – **Proactive**	Has a significant degree of IM maturity. Enterprise awareness, policies, procedures and standards exist and are generally utilized across all enterprise projects. At level 3, the IM practices are typically sponsored and managed by IT
Level 4 - **Managed**	Manages information as an enterprise asset. The business is heavily engaged in IM procedures and takes responsibility for the quality of information that they manage. A level 4 organization has many mature and best-in-class practices and utilizes audits to ensure compliance across all projects
Level 5 - **Optimized**	Considers information to be as much an enterprise asset as financial and material assets. A level 5 organization has best-in-class IM practices that are utilized across all enterprise projects. The distinguishing characteristic of a level 5 organization is the focus on continuous improvement. At level 5, all data management practices and assets are regularly measured and the results are analyzed as the basis for process improvement

Source: MIKE2.0 (www.openmethodology.org).

The assessment also allows the organization to analyze the details for each domain. For example, the organization was interested in looking at the details for the technology category. The technology category is further broken down and assessed according to a number of functional areas and each is assigned its own score (see Figure 3.4). Each functional area for Technology Management has been described in Table 3.2. The functional areas actually reveal some of the reasons for technology score being at reactive level even in the presence of enterprise-wide systems. The scores for Profiling/Measurement, Metadata Management, Data Stewardship and Data Capture, all of which are important for harnessing the value from the data, are all weak. This again highlights the importance of the Information Maturity Assessment before investing significantly in analytics because no matter how much is invested in the analytics, if

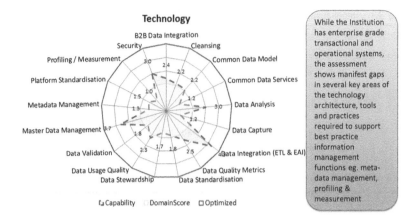

Figure 3.4   Technology assessment.

Table 3.2   Definition of Technology Functional Areas

FUNCTIONAL AREA	DESCRIPTION
B2B data integration	Is data received from, or sent to, other organizations consistently handled?
Cleansing	Are data cleansing tools appropriately deployed?
Common data model	Considers the use of consistent data models and standards
Common data services	Use of middleware and standard messages to interface data between systems
Data analysis	Extent to which data analysis technologies are appropriately deployed
Data capture	Considers the use of consistent design approaches to collecting data from end users or customers
Data integration	Are automated data integration tools used (as opposed to inconsistent manual coding)?
Data quality metrics	Considers the inclusion of automated data quality metrics
Data standardization	Extent to which data integration is combined with technology to standardize data (such as capitalizing names, splitting fields etc.)
Data stewardship	Provision of monitoring technology for data quality and other management metrics
Data usage quality	Extent of utilization of the primary data assets by end users for their decision-making
Data validation	Consistent use of rules to validate data entered or supplied
Master data management	Use of common platforms to manage master data across the organization
Metadata management	Appropriate technology to manage and disseminate metadata
Platform standardization	Extent to which data management forms part of the technology platform strategy
Profiling/measurement	Is a data profiling technology consistently used?
Security	Technology management of data aspects of security

these technology functional areas are not improved the benefits will not be realized.

The institution's investment in transactional and operational systems resulted in Technology being assessed the highest of the six domains, however, the weaknesses in policy, people and practices limit the effectiveness of the IT investments. This perspective will enable business leadership to look beyond the technical issues to identify and address the critical areas of attention if it is to realize greater value from its data assets and information resources.

Aggregating the same assessment results using the IBM-DGCMM dimensions (see Figure 3.5) reflects very clearly where the strengths and weaknesses of the organization lie within its Enterprise Information Management capabilities. The result of this alternative assessment is illustrated in Figure 3.5. This perspective reinforces the earlier insights derived from the IM Assessment. The institution is not creating/realizing maximum value from its data/information assets and requires greater attention to organizational enablers such as improved Information Governance practices in Data ownership and stewardship. Executive management needs to signal the importance of BI through more effective messaging, policy and organizational mechanisms (roles/responsibilities).

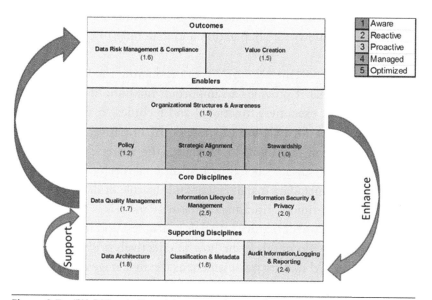

Figure 3.5   IBM-DGC maturity model assessment perspective.

The findings of the IM Assessment are discussed, with both functional and technology participants, and validated using key stakeholder workshops. The results are reconciled with the outcomes of semi-structured interviews that are conducted in parallel. This typically provides a qualitative consistency to support the quantitative assessment scores. The granularity of the IM Assessment will enable the organization to program the development of a balanced portfolio of BI initiatives that will include technology and applications projects, as well as capacity building/training, organizational structures/roles and policy initiatives. Additionally, the granularity provides an important medium of engagement for executive, functional and technology management to collaborate in the formulation of a strategic BI Roadmap.

Conclusion

In this chapter, we posit that an IM maturity assessment is an important foundational step that is both agile and resource-efficient and will enable organizations to assess and benchmark their Enterprise Information Management capabilities as a precursor to formulating a strategic, agile BI strategy.

The AIMS-BI IM maturity model supported by the assessment instrument is flexible to adaptation and use in various types of organizations. This allows for adaptability and matching to the context of SMEs.

One of the important "*intangibles*" of conducting the IM Maturity Assessment is that it provides an important medium of engagement and dialogue for executive, functional and technical management to collaborate in the formulation of strategic BI initiatives. This facilitated dialogue can highlight, for instance, the shared responsibility for data quality assurance including institutional mechanisms such as data standards, metadata management and the role of data stewards.

One of the common criticisms of maturity models is that whereas the primary purpose of maturity models is to assess and identify capability gaps, many do not describe how to effectively address the gaps identified. The IM maturity assessment as the first stage of AIMS-BI embeds the IM assessment in an integrated development process that addresses this significant "*knowing-doing*" gap.

4

CREATING BI PORTFOLIOS

Most of us spend too much time on what is urgent and not enough time on what is important.

Stephen R. Covey

Introduction

The second and the third steps of AIMS-BI involve discovering and prioritizing BI opportunities in order to create a *prioritized BI portfolio* of possible Proof of Concepts (PoCs) initiatives. This need for a prioritized portfolio is based on the premise that it is unlikely that organizations, especially SMEs, have the resources to address all BI opportunities at once. AIMS-BI allows organizations to build and evaluate a portfolio of BI initiatives to identify those that are perceived as likely to provide the greatest strategic value to the organization. This chapter describes how these initiatives can be identified and prioritized, then, depending on the resources available and the resources needed for each, the top initiatives can be selected for implementation as PoCs.

The development of this prioritized portfolio requires an understanding of the stakeholder needs and identifying possible opportunities for the organization in terms of strategic BI. It is important to gain a thorough understanding of the organization's business, assess any current BI initiatives that the organizations have in place or are planning to invest in, and discover BI opportunities that align with the strategic initiatives of the organization.

The Discovery of BI Opportunities

The aim of this step is to identify a set of strategic BI opportunities for the organization. In order to ensure the completeness of this set, multiple stakeholders (e.g. business leaders, business analysts and data analysts) across several functional areas of the organization should be engaged. This early engagement of stakeholders adds agility to the methodology.

The engagement of the stakeholders is done using semi-structured interviews and the objectives of these interviews are to: (i) gain a more thorough understanding of the organization's business; (ii) assess current BI initiatives; (iii) understand any planned BI investments; and (iv) discover BI opportunities. Discovering BI opportunities must be done within the context of the specific organization, so the interviews are used to assess the current situation of the organization including identifying existing resources, understanding the constraints and identifying business success criteria. In parallel with understanding what exists within the organization, an understanding of what other comparable organizations have achieved through the adoption of BI initiatives and the critical success factors they have identified are extremely important considerations. This consideration of the achievements of others allows the organization to be clear, not just about what they should invest in, but, just as importantly, what others, globally, have done successfully. This global perspective can be achieved by referring to existing case studies. The information from the interviews together with the findings from the analysis of the case studies are then used to develop the organization's portfolio of BI initiatives.

In order to better understand the value of each initiative to the organization, further information is elicited from the stakeholders. This additional information includes:

- the name of the initiative
- the type of BI involved (e.g. advanced vs descriptive analytics)
- the business process it supports
- the target users
- the business context
- the strategic objective the initiative aligns with
- the consumers of the information
- key business questions the initiative will answer
- the performance measures
- the constraints (i.e. what will affect the success of the initiative; e.g. poor data quality)
- the data sources needed to implement the initiative.

Figure 4.1 Inputs to BI portfolio.

An online form can be developed to collect this information and follow-up interviews can be used to clarify this information. All the information gathered is used to create the portfolio of Proof of Concepts (PoCs). The inputs into the development of the portfolio are summarized in Figure 4.1.

BI Portfolio Evaluation

When a portfolio of PoC initiatives has been created using the guidelines above, it may be necessary to *prioritize* the initiatives given the likelihood of limited resources. It may be the case that some of the PoCs are mandatory as they are prerequisites to the success of the other initiatives. For example, based on the IM Maturity Assessment (see Chapter 3) and the discussions with the stakeholders, the issue of data quality may keep reoccurring. Given that the success of the initiatives is likely to be highly dependent on the quality of the data, it may have to be agreed that a data quality PoC is mandatory. The remaining PoCs would then be prioritized to help in determining which should be developed into prototypes.

Different stakeholders will have their own preferences as to which PoCs are most important and there are a number of criteria to consider in this prioritization process. A subjective, multi-criteria decision-making technique is suited to this process. Based on these needs, the multi-criteria decision making technique, Analytic Hierarchical Processing (AHP) (Saaty, 1980), can be used as it is specially designed for multi-criteria, subjective estimation. AHP uses a hierarchical structure with a *goal*, a set of *alternatives* that are to be prioritized and the set of *criteria* that need to be considered in the prioritization. In this case, the *goal* is the prioritization of the PoCs in the portfolio, the *alternatives* are the possible PoCs and the *criteria* are the strategic objectives of the organization. Using the strategic objectives as the criteria against which the PoCs should be assessed ensures the alignment of the BI agenda with that of the strategy of the organization. The pairwise comparison of the alternatives in relation to each of the criteria is done by the stakeholders using the ranking guide in Table 4.1.

The criteria themselves can also be prioritized based on their importance to the organization. The pairwise comparison combines the criteria importance with the alternative preference measure to derive a numerical priority for each solution alternative. This approach checks the ranking's consistency in the pairwise comparison to ensure that the comparison is being done in a consistent manner. The output from applying AHP will be the portfolio of PoCs with a numerical priority for each. This priority rating is used to identify those PoCs that will provide the greatest impact in terms of achieving the strategic objectives and therefore should be where the limited resources should be invested.

The selected PoCs are to be signed off by the PoC sponsors (i.e. the senior manager(s) under whom the PoC falls). The inclusion of the stakeholders in the prioritization process as well as the alignment of each initiative with a strategic objective supports the agility of the proposed methodology.

Table 4.1   Ranking Guide

COMPARED TO THE SECOND ALTERNATIVE, THE FIRST ALTERNATIVE IS:	NUMERICAL RATING
Extremely preferred	9
	8
Very strongly preferred	7
	6
Strongly preferred	5
	4
Moderately preferred	3
	2
Equally Preferred	1

Example: BI Opportunity Discovery and Portfolio Evaluation

To demonstrate the opportunity discovery and portfolio evaluation steps we use the example of a financial institution. The IM assessment was performed and was followed up with the semi-structured interviews which provided a better understanding of the state of the organization's BI agenda. The main strategic objectives of the organization were also elicited in these discussions. They were framed on Sales, Payments, Efficiency and Service. The information gathered at this stage is critical for the alignment of the PoCs with the strategy of the organization.

An example portfolio of PoCs for a financial institution is described in Table 4.2. For each of the possible BI initiatives, a brief description and the strategic objective it aligns with have been provided.

Through discussions with senior management, the set of BI initiatives was reduced to a number of possible PoCs. Based on the current needs, some of these PoCs were considered mandatory and some were

Table 4.2 Example Portfolio of PoCs

	PoC	PoC DESCRIPTION	STRATEGIC OBJECTIVE
1	Market segmentation	This PoC demonstrates analytics models/techniques that can be used to segment the customer market	Sales
2	Credit risk analysis	This PoC demonstrates the use of analytics modeling techniques (e.g. decision trees) for credit risk analysis. It is likely that financial institutions are already doing some risk analysis but this PoC demonstrates the importance of considering alternative models	Sales, payments
3	Call center traffic pattern analysis	Analysis of call center data set: • To determine how the call center operators are performing (e.g. length of time to process various requests) • To show the traffic at the call center at various times which can then be used to determine the optimal allocation of call center resources	Efficiency, service
4	Market Basket analysis	Identification of products that sell well together and can help to increase the effectiveness of sales campaign management and targeting processes (e.g. cross-sell and upsell of products)	Sales
5	Customer segment value analysis	Many organizations have found that a small percentage of customers contribute the majority of the value to the organization. Therefore this PoC calculates the profitability or lifetime value of customers and show the changes that occur as the customers move through the lifecycle (e.g. from low profitability through medium to high)	Sales, service

(Continued)

Table 4.2 (*Continued*)   Example Portfolio of PoCs

	PoC	PoC DESCRIPTION	STRATEGIC OBJECTIVE
6	Segmentation & credit risk analysis of the semi-banked	It is easier to market to existing rather than new customers, therefore, this PoC will analyze customer data to identify ways to get more value from the semi-banked	Sales, payments
7	Banking distribution channel analysis and optimization	Each distribution channel has a cost associated with it and there are benefits of moving customers across channels. This PoC can also assist in allocating resources (e.g. identifying where new ATMs/branches should be located)	Efficiency, service
8	Sales performance management dashboard	Develops sales performance dashboards that provide members of staff with interactive drill-down visibility for sales performance across the enterprise	Sales
9	Payments analytics	Explores the use of payments data for customer analytics to determine how payments can provide additional predictor variables for credit-risk scoring or customer segmentation	Payments
10	Data quality analytics on customer data	Demonstrates the importance of data profiling and how it can be used to assess and improve the quality of organizational data. Data quality is one of the most significant factors affecting the success of data-driven initiatives	Sales, efficiency, service
11	Data integration/ data as a service	Identifies benefits and issues of data integration and demonstrates techniques for improving data accessibility. It highlights the importance of data standardization to the integration process. It demonstrates that appropriate data governance and standardization policies can lead to significant improvements in the efficiency of decision-making	Efficiency
12	Visual analysis with Tableau workshop	A key goal of agile analytics is to provide decision-makers with the tools to access data and direct their own analysis. The organization had *Tableau*, a popular and powerful analytics/data visualization tool, but it is was being used extensively	Efficiency

thought to be important for short-term consideration. For example, Data Quality is foundational to the success of analytics initiatives but it was clear from the IM assessment and interviews that there were data quality issues that could hamper BI and therefore the Data Quality PoC was considered to be mandatory. Another mandatory PoC was Data as a Service (DaaS) as this provides the ability to integrate data on a need-be basis. Four other PoCs that the organization identified as important in the short term were Market Basket Analysis, Payment Analytics, Distribution Channel Optimization,

Segmentation and Credit Risk of Semi-Banked. It was agreed, however, given the availability and access to resources and the need for a quick turnaround, that only two of these four should be developed as prototypes.

A larger team was constituted to select the top two PoCs for development. The inclusion of key decision-makers across various functional areas as a part of this selection team ensures further buy-in and agility in the methodology and the outcome. The subjective multi-criteria group decision-making technique, AHP, was used for this prioritization process.

This prioritization process was extremely participatory. At a half-day workshop the stakeholders were briefed on the findings from the application of AIMS-BI to date and were asked to prioritize the remaining initiatives based on the impact each would have on the strategic directions e.g. (i) Credit Expansion (ii) Sales and Service (iii) Efficiency (iv) Payments (see Figure 4.2).

The stakeholders were grouped and each group was asked to do a comparison of each pair of alternatives with respect to the criteria using the ranking guide shown in Table 4.1. For an example template see Figure 4.3.

The criteria themselves could have also been ranked, however, in this case, they were assumed to have equal importance. On completion of the pairwise ranking, the rankings were normalized and used to compute a score for each of the alternatives with respect to each of these criteria. These scores were then combined to derive an overall score for each alternative, which was then used to prioritize the PoCs (see Table 4.3). In the example, Market Basket Analysis and

Criteria	
C1	**Credit Expansion** - penetration opportunities, product push through right-fit offers, efficient delivery
C2	**Sales & Service** - extend wallet share, engaging value proposals, customer satisfaction
C3	**Efficiency** - process improvement, agility
C4	**Payments** - extend competitive advantage, lead digitization
Alternatives	
A1	Payment Analytics
A2	Distribution Channel Optimisation
A3	Segmentation and Credit Risk of Semi-Banked
A4	Market Basket

Figure 4.2 Criteria and alternatives.

Ranking by C1 - Credit Expansion

	A1	A2	A3	A4
A1	1.00	8.00	9.00	1.00
A2	0.13	1.00	0.13	0.11
A3	0.11	8.00	1.00	0.11
A4	1.00	9.00	9.00	1.00

Ranking by C2 - Sales & Service

	A1	A2	A3	A4
A1	1.00	8.00	4.00	0.33
A2	0.13	1.00	0.20	0.11
A3	0.25	5.00	1.00	0.17
A4	3.00	9.00	6.00	1.00

Ranking by C4 - Payments

	A1	A2	A3	A4
A1	1.00	6.00	1.00	3.00
A2	0.17	1.00	4.00	3.00
A3	1.00	0.25	1.00	2.00
A4	0.33	0.33	0.50	1.00

Ranking by C3 - Efficiency

	A1	A2	A3	A4
A1	1.00	0.13	0.14	0.13
A2	8.00	1.00	7.00	5.00
A3	7.00	0.14	1.00	0.14
A4	8.00	0.20	7.00	1.00

Figure 4.3   AHP pairwise comparison.

Table 4.3   AHP Ranking of PoCs

ALTERNATIVE	POC	RANKING
A4	Market Basket	1
A1	Payment Analytics	2
A2	Distribution Channel Optimization	3
A3	Segmentation and Credit Risk of Semi-Banked	4

Payments Analytics were the two chosen for the development of analytics prototypes.

Conclusion

The process of the development and prioritization of BI initiatives proved to be extremely participatory especially when it came to applying the prioritization process. There were very lively discussions and active participation in applying the AHP. The buy-in from stakeholders as well as the alignment of the initiatives with the strategic objectives of the organization ensures that the BI agenda is transformational. Thus, the chapter highlights the importance of engaging key stakeholders in building this portfolio of initiatives as this contributes to the agility of the AIMS-BI methodology.

5

THE PROCESS AND VALUE OF BUILDING PROOF-OF-CONCEPT PROTOTYPES

If you can't describe what you are doing as a process, you don't know what you're doing.

W. Edwards Deming

Introduction

AIMS-BI consists of four steps which lead to the development of a strategic Business Intelligence (BI) roadmap, tailored to the organization's business context and capabilities. This chapter focuses on Step 4 which involves developing the prototypes for the selected Proof of Concepts (PoCs). The prototypes serve several purposes including securing the buy-in of executive management and providing a more thorough understanding of the amount of time and resources that will have to be invested in a full-blown BI implementation. The prototypes are also integral to the development of the BI roadmap as they help to identify those key areas on which the organization needs to focus and develop capabilities if it is to maximize the benefits of its investment in a BI strategy. The agile methodology requires a quick, low-cost, turnaround development of the prototypes which can be achieved using open source solutions. However, many organizations may not have the resources and expertise to developing the PoCs effectively and therefore end up building them in a rather ad hoc way. In this chapter, we discuss the existing process models that can be adopted to ensure that the development of PoCs is done is a systematic structured way.

Why Develop PoCs?

Davenport and Harris (2007) provide many exemplars of organizations that make widespread use of BI and Data Assets to create significant value for them by employing an enterprise approach with strong senior management advocacy and leadership. The authors propose a path that organizations need to traverse to reach an "Analytics Competitor" state in which the organization begins to consistently realize a stream of rich insights from BI that translates into actionable value. As illustrated in Figure 5.1, reaching this state typically requires navigating through a critical stage 2 in which functional analytics initiatives are used to build momentum and secure executive interest. Empirical evidence suggests that many enterprise BI initiatives stall at this point, which might be characterized as a *"chasm of uncertainty"*, and never make it to stage 3, where there is executive commitment and resource allocation to a strategic BI vision. AIMS-BI provides a systematic and rapid approach to navigating these first three stages and producing a strategic BI roadmap that reflects the key BI opportunities and a visible program of implementation. The organization will then be positioned

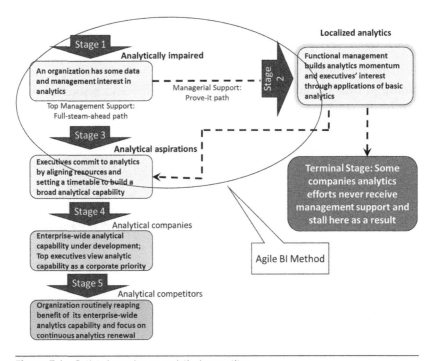

Figure 5.1   Path to becoming an analytical competitor.

to secure executive commitment and the resources required to put it on the path to becoming a serious "Analytics Competitor".

BI – The Different Layers of Analytics

The various layers of analytics (see Figure 5.2) include reporting, analysis, monitoring and prediction. The techniques available in each layer answer specific types of questions. The lowest level, the Reporting level, focuses on "What happened?" questions and so includes techniques that facilitate querying and searching (e.g. SQL). The next layer up is the Analysis layer which focuses on the question "Why did it happen?" and allows the decision-makers to view the data from multiple dimensions using Online Analytical Processing (OLAP) and data visualization tools. The next layer, the Monitoring layer, focuses on the question "What is happening now?" and uses tools such as dashboards and scorecards. The Prediction layer looks into the future to answer the question "What might happen?" which requires data mining techniques and tools. Finally, the Prescription layer is about finding appropriate actions, based on the results of the prediction combined with the decision-makers' business insights, to ensure the benefits of BI initiatives.

The techniques and technologies recommended to answer the question related to each layer should not be applied in an ad hoc way, but

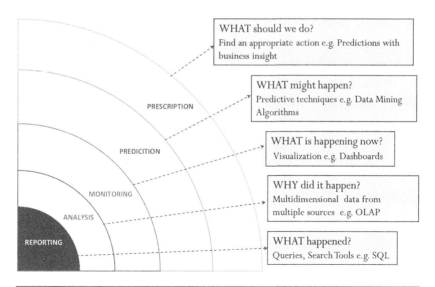

Figure 5.2 Layers of analytics.

should follow one of the process models that have been used to build BI initiatives. Such models provide a systematic and focused approach to the development of the BI PoCs. The following section discusses the application of models to the *Monitoring* and the *Prediction* layers.

Monitoring Layer

The monitoring layer is focused on the question of "What is Happening Now?" and to answer this question Visualization techniques and technologies are recommended.

What Is Data Visualization?

Data visualization is a technique that allows information and data to be represented in a graphical or pictorial format. Data can often be overwhelming and difficult to process and since "a picture is worth a thousand words", visualization is used to simplify it. Visualizations can take varying formats from key measures being presented to the executives each morning, to big screens that show real-time data, such as statistics in a graphical manner, to interactive charts/graphs that allow the user to explore the data. Data visualizations are used to tell stories through the use of the many available visuals (e.g. charts, graphs, images, text) connected in a cohesive and coordinated manner. They not only allow decision-makers to see the complete picture as it emerges from the data, but also allow a level of interactivity across the visuals to explore how changes in one visual may affect the others.

Visualizations are built to narrate the stories that exist in data i.e. "What is happening now?" The insights from data are often lost if they are not explained to the decision-makers. Visualizations use graphics to translate large volumes of data to insights which can be used to make informed decisions and converted into actions. The data visualization process should follow a model to ensure that it is done in a systematic and structured way.

Data Visualization Process Models (VPM)

Process models, generally, provide a systematic, repeatable set of steps to guide decision-makers. The Data Visualization Process Model (see Figure 5.3), in particular, outlines the steps that decision-makers should follow when implementing a Data Visualization initiative. The VPM model starts with an *understanding of the business context* and ends with the *enabling of decision-making and actions*. To understand the business context those KPIs that affect the business objective are first determined and then used to help identify the variables in the data set that should be considered. To see how the variables are performing, various graphs and charts are generated and finally the designer needs to ensure that the visualizations are assisting with some decision or action. Each of the steps is described below:

Understanding the Business Context
This step requires that the analyst identifies the business questions that are to be answered by the visualization. Not only do these business questions need to be identified, but it is also important that the analyst understands the audience (i.e. the decision-maker) for whom the visualization is being developed. To understand the audience,

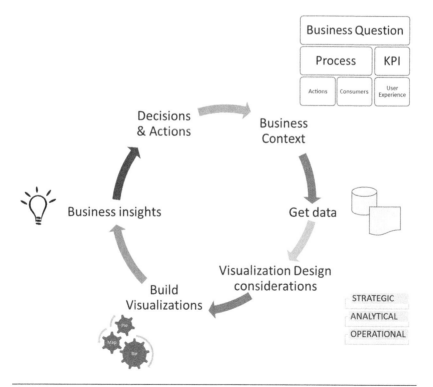

Figure 5.3 Data visualization process model.

the analyst needs to interact with the business user and identify the *story* that needs to be told through the visualization. Numbers convey a powerful message; therefore the important metrics will need to be identified. A good starting point for identifying these metrics is the organization's Key Performance Indicators (KPIs) as these metrics align with strategic objectives and measure actual performance against targets, thresholds and timelines. KPIs are critical to any performance management system so they need to be incorporated in the dashboards or stories of the visualization. Also these metrics should be represented in the visualizations as many leaders recognize that *"What gets measured gets done"* and so the inclusion of the KPIs in the visualization will improve accountability. The business questions should focus on the following aspects of the organization:

- *What* – e.g. what are the best-selling products?
- *When* – e.g. at what times of the year do the sales of a certain product spike?
- *Where* – e.g. in which regions/countries is a particular product doing best?
- *As compared to* – e.g. how are the sales of Brand X's 50 mL water compared to Brand Y's over the last 3 months?
- *By how much* – e.g. what is the percentage increase in the sales of Product X over the last 3 months?

Get Data

Having identified the key business questions and metrics for the visualization, the next step is to identify and retrieve the data needed to do the visualization. It is likely that this data resides in disparate sources throughout the organization, and some may even be external. Therefore, identified data items will need to be integrated. As a part of this integration process, the issue of data preparation and cleansing will have to be addressed. In terms of preparation, some visuals may require the data to be in a different format to the one it is stored in at the source so the data will have to be transformed into a form suited to the visualization. Additionally, any quality issues with the source data must be resolved before it is included in the data for the visualization. Chapters 6 and 7 provide details of both data integration and data cleaning and preparation.

Visualization Design Considerations
To design and build effective visualizations the following questions need to be considered:

1. How will the user respond to the visualization?
2. How will the visualization be used?
3. How should the data be encoded?

How Will the User Respond to the Visualization?
The user experience can be on three levels, namely:

- Visceral – the visceral experience relates to a quick emotional reaction. This feeling is more intuitive than rational and involves the basic perceptual tasks of distinguishing objects and is really about forming the true first impression.
- Behavioral – this experience is about conscious awareness and is controlled by cognition but influenced by visceral reaction. This is the level of most human behavior.
- Reflective – this experience is solely a cognitive and intellectual response; it is not influenced by the visceral reaction.

How Will the Visualization Be Used?
Visualizations and Dashboards can be used for many levels of decision-making e.g. strategic, analytical or operational decisions. The narrative will differ depending on the use of the visualization.

Strategic Dashboards – monitor the execution of corporate strategic objectives at each level of the organization and emphasize management rather than monitoring or analysis. They are often implemented using the Balanced Scorecard methodology and are referred to as *scorecards*.

Analytic Dashboards – track departmental processes and projects and emphasize analysis rather than monitoring or management. They are often implemented using portals and run against data marts or warehouses where data is refreshed periodically.

Operational Dashboards – track core operational processes and often display real-time data. Operational dashboards emphasize monitoring more than analysis or management.

How Should the Data Be Encoded?

The various dimensions of data can be encoded with appropriate visual properties. There are a number of options for data encoding including color, size, shape, spatial position, length, width and orientation, and the selection of these options is extremely important for the effectiveness of the visual. For example, colors bring out people's emotions, so for a visualization that is narrating murder rates the color red automatically heightens the emotive response. Colors also simplify complexity. In a complex graphical encoding color can draw attention to one detail while blurring others; it can be used to highlight or alert the user to some particular event that was discovered in the data. Colors can be monotone where the ordering shows low to high concept (e.g. number of customers in different regions), they can be diverging with the use of two colors and a neutral color e.g. (profit – low, zero, high), or they can be contrasting to highlight comparisons (e.g. difference between sales and profit). The choice and amount of color should be considered carefully as too much color can make the visualization confusing.

The encoding choice is dependent on the data type as particular types are suited to particular codings as depicted in Table 5.1.

These options, when used in combination, can be extremely effective for developing the narrative.

The design questions for visualizations (i.e. how will users respond? how will the visualization be used? and how should data be encoded?) are intricately intertwined. For example, the user's response to the visualization can be influenced by the data encoding while the visualization can be designed to elicit a specific response. Since the design for a visceral experience seeks to generate a quick affective emotional reaction, analysts use color and size to elicit this reaction, for example,

Table 5.1 Type of Data and their Encoding

CATEGORICAL DATA	ORDINAL DATA	QUANTITATIVE DATA
Position	Position	Position
Color hues	Size	Length
Shape	Color intensity	Size
Clusters	Color hues	Color intensity
Boundaries	Shapes	-

red and big can be used to represent a highly dramatic narrative. The behavioral experience focuses on issues such as readability and usability. These visualizations are interactive in nature and allow users to literally have a *conversation with the data*. Analytical dashboards will have a higher degree of interactivity whereas strategic dashboards, which present highly summarized data primarily for senior management decision-makers, require little interactivity. A reflective user experience occurs in visualizations when the graphics result in decisions and/or actions. Operational dashboards should be action-oriented and strategic dashboards should be decision-oriented. Using size and color for key variables on strategic dashboards will tend to focus the attention of the decision-makers on the key performance indicators. All these aspects of the design need to be considered in order to ensure that the visualization is fit for its purpose and also geared toward the specific decision-makers.

Building Visualizations
In building visualizations, the data is encoded as a visual object with multiple components. The analysts will have to select visualization techniques and group the individual visualizations to form a strong narrative. The business questions, the data and the design considerations will be used to create the individual graphical encodings. For example, if the focus of an organization is on customer satisfaction, the analyst will need to graphically encode the current customer satisfaction levels, customer satisfaction across branches/regions, the trend of customer satisfaction over years and quarters, the relationship between sales and customer satisfaction etc. For each graph the analyst will have to determine the most appropriate representation (i.e. bar, pie, line, heat map) and connect them so that the big picture emerges.

Business Insights
The visualizations enable decision-makers to gain evidence-based insights into the organization. They interact with the visualizations to derive insights based on the compelling stories that emerge from the graphics. The graphical, summarized and multiple views of the data enable the decision-makers to understand the complete picture that is embedded within data.

Decisions and Actions

This step allows the analyst to share insights with other stakeholders through views, dashboards and stories. These insights are then used to drive business actions and make more data-driven decisions. The impact of the visualization will be realized when the decisions and/or actions are reflected in improvements to Key Performance Indicators (KPI) of the organization. The visualizations may explain some of the mysteries embedded in the data which will guide new business questions.

Prediction Layer

The prediction layer of analytics is focused on the question "What Might Happen?" To answer this question, data mining techniques and tools are recommended. Again, a process model for data mining should be followed to ensure that the required steps are taken in a systematic and structured way.

What Is Data Mining?

Data mining has been defined as the process of extracting valid, non-trivial, previously unknown, interesting patterns or associations from large databases. It is routinely being used in marketing, retail, banking, telecommunications, supply chain optimization and fraud detection applications.

The data mining techniques can be classified as either predictive or descriptive. Predictive techniques are considered to be supervised learning methods as they require a labeled training set. Labeled means that there is a training set for which there is a known value for a target variable. For example, if customers are to be classified as *high* or *low* risk there is a target variable (e.g. *risk level*) and a training set of customer data for which their value for the *risk level* variable are known to be either *high* or *low*. The technique is then used to build a model which identifies those input variables that are important in predicting the given target variable and so focuses on either classifying data into a set of predefined classes (i.e. one for each possible value for the target variable) or predicting future data states for that target variable. When a new case is presented for which there is no value for the target variable (i.e. the class it belongs to is not known), the model is used to predict the class. Examples of predictive analytic techniques are classification, regression and value prediction.

Classification is the most commonly applied data mining technique in predictive modeling. It consists of three stages: model construction, model evaluation and model use. It uses a set of pre-classified examples (i.e. training data set) to develop a model that can classify the population in the future. In the model construction or learning phase the training data is used by the selected classification algorithm to build a classifier model. In the evaluation phase the generated model is checked for accuracy using test or validation data and, if the model is acceptable, it is used to classify new data. Common classification algorithms include decision trees, logistic regression, k-NN and neural networks.

Descriptive techniques, on the other hand, are unsupervised learning methods. They do not have a test data set with a known target variable, rather they focus on describing behavior. Common descriptive techniques include sequence mining and association rule mining.

Association rule induction is a commonly used technique in data analytics which is used to find recurring patterns in data of the form $X => Y$ (i.e. X implies Y), where X and Y are concepts or sets of concepts which frequently occur together in the data set. Association rules have been used successfully for market basket analysis which is based on the theory that if a customer buys a certain group of items, they are more (or less) likely to buy another group of items. It is a technique that has become extremely popular in the retail business and to understand customers purchase behaviors and to identify relationships between the items that people buy. The generation of association rules is a two-step process. First all the itemsets, where each itemset is a set of items a customer buys in one transaction, that satisfy a user-specified minimum support criterion are extracted from the data set. The associations between the items that occur frequently together are then identified using a user-specified minimum confidence criterion. The two criteria, confidence and minimum support, are significant as they generate a large number of possible association rules and therefore require techniques that are able to identify the most *useful* ones.

As it is unlikely that there is only one possible data mining technique that can be applied to a given data set, choosing which are the most appropriate for a given problem and a given data set is not a trivial task. Therefore, it is important that this choice is guided by a multiphase knowledge discovery process model such as IKDDM – Integrated Knowledge Discovery and Data Mining.

IKDDM Process Model for Data Mining

The need for formal data mining process models that prescribe a path from data to knowledge discovery has been recognized. These models provide a framework that allows for the identification of all the inputs and outputs associated with tasks as well as their dependencies within and across the phases of the process. Following such a process model provides a mechanism for applying data mining techniques in a systematic and structured manner thereby increasing the likelihood that the results will be accurate and reliable and the process is repeatable.

One such process model is the IKDDM model (see Figure 5.4) which consists of the following phases: Business (or Application Domain) Understanding (which includes definition of business and data mining goals), Data Understanding, Data Preparation, Data Mining/Analytics (or Modeling), Evaluation (evaluation of results based on Data Mining goals) and Deployment. Each of these phases is described below:

Business Understanding Phase

This first phase focuses on the project objectives and requirements from a business perspective, understanding them fully and then converting this knowledge into a Data Mining problem definition. A preliminary plan for achieving the project objectives should be developed.

Data Understanding

This phase starts with an initial data collection and proceeds to activities which familiarize analysts with the data and allow them to identify data quality problems, to discover first insights into the data or to detect interesting subsets to form hypotheses for hidden information.

Data Preparation

This phase covers all activities associated with constructing the final data set (data that will be fed into the modeling tool(s)) from the initial

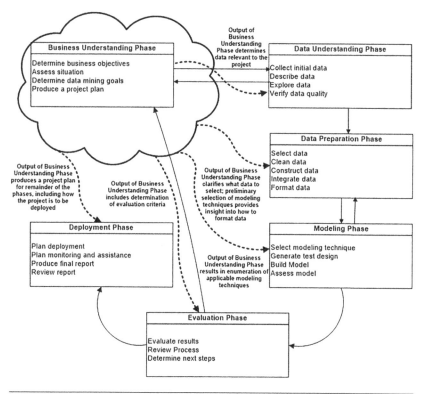

Figure 5.4 Phases of the IKDDM model (Sharma and Osei-Bryson, 2010).

raw data. Data preparation tasks are likely to be performed multiple times and not in any prescribed order. These activities include table, record and attribute selection as well as the transformation and cleaning of data.

Modeling (Data Mining)
In this phase, various modeling techniques (e.g. Decision Trees, Regression and Clustering) are selected and applied. Typically, there are several techniques that could be applied to a given problem type and some of these techniques have specific requirements in terms of the format of the data that is needed to perform them, therefore, this phase often requires repeating the data preparation phase.

Evaluation
This phase of the project consists of thoroughly evaluating the model and reviewing the steps executed to construct the model to be certain that it properly achieves the business objectives. A key objective is to

determine if there is some important business issue that has not been sufficiently considered. At the end of this phase, a decision on the use of the Data Mining results should be reached.

Deployment

The creation of the model is not the end of the process as simply extracting the knowledge from the data is of little value if it is not organized and presented in a way that the decision-makers can use of it. The deployment can be as simple as generating a report or as complex as implementing a repeatable Data Mining process across the enterprise. It is important that the decision-makers are clear about the actions that they can take to make use of the models.

**Lessons Learned from Applying the Process
Models to the Development of the PoCs**

The development of the PoCs using the established process model of IKDDM or VPM as presented in the case studies have led to several key insights. First, modeling is an iterative not a linear process. In IKDDM the iterations between the business understanding and data understanding phases improve the understanding of the data that is required to fulfill the business objective. These iterations help to identify the data required, the missing data and the dirty data and lead to the selection of the appropriate input variables and target variables, and the creation of derived variables. The iteration between data preparation and modeling, is critical for obtaining relevant results from the modeling phase. These iterations could include modifying the measurement levels of the variable as these levels could impact the activities in the modeling phase. However, analysts need to be mindful that some iterations between other phases will make the process inefficient and costly so they must be considered carefully.

Second, data preparation/get data is a non-trivial, often underestimated activity, especially when working with data from disparate sources. Often the absence of business rules for the domain obfuscates the process of data preparation and the creation of new variables. The data preparation/get data phase is reliant on the knowledge and experience of the data analysts, especially their understanding of the relationship between business objectives and the data required to achieve these objectives.

Third, the validation and the business value assessment of a model are functions of technical knowledge of model parameters and business domain expertise and interpretation. This insight underscores the critical importance and the role of business analysts working in collaboration with data analysts and BI analysts. Collaboration between the three is essential and informs the business analyst in the deployment phase of the process models in IKDDM and the business insights phase of VPM.

Fourth, organizations need to emphasize data quality management strategies and improve their data quality and metadata as part of a portfolio of BI initiatives. Data quality is multidimensional in nature and includes the format, accuracy, presence, meaning and relatedness of field-level data. Assessing data quality on multiple dimensions is difficult and therefore it is important that the organization adopts master data management as this provides a single point of reference for critical organizational data which ensures that everyone understands and interprets the data in the same way. Data quality is an important issue as poor data can undermine the generated knowledge.

Conclusion

Data is seen as one of an organization's most valuable assets and finding innovative ways to harness value from it can create a strategic advantage for the organization. The move toward data-driven decision-making is an indication that organizations have started to leverage the opportunities presented by their data and that data is central to decision-making contexts.

The availability of a process model for the development of PoCs and full-blown analytics initiatives will provide guidance to organizations that are new to the field and those that may not have a great deal of experience in applying analytics effectively.

6

DATA GOVERNANCE AND
DATA QUALITY MANAGEMENT

Quality is not an act, it is a habit

Aristotle

Introduction

Data Quality and Data Governance have been identified as two factors that have constrained the efficiency and effectiveness of data-driven analytics initiatives and decision-making processes. The Information Management Maturity assessment, administered in the first step of AIMS-BI, rates both Data Quality (DQ) and Data Governance and highlights issues surrounding them. Beyond the obvious issue of accuracy (i.e. degree to which data values are correct), inconsistent data formats, missing values, same field names with different meanings from different data sources, and the identification of logical relatedness between specific data instances based on values are all commonly occurring issues that highlight the need for a systematic approach to DQ. Additionally, even if current DQ issues are addressed, without proper Data Governance and the accountability and ownership it provides, these errors will reoccur.

This chapter outlines what both Data Governance and DQ entail, explains why they are critical to Business Intelligence (BI) and then goes on to describe, in detail, a systematic approach to DQ standards definition and DQ measurement. The chapter will also demonstrate the use of DQ Dashboards for empowering data stewards in formulating and overseeing adherence to DQ standards and policies across the organization. The emphasis will also be on the systemic approaches to measurement, ranking and quantification of DQ and asset value and how these can be maintained through proper Data Governance practices.

Data Governance and Data Quality

Data Governance is a set of processes and practices that are established to support the formal management of data assets within the organization. Its aim is to establish consistent DQ, improve data integrity, control data access and address data security and retention. These processes and practices are used to manage the execution and enforcement of authority over the definition, production and usage of data and data-related resources.

Data Governance covers a number of areas that help the organization to gain better control over its data assets, including DQ, Data Stewardship, Security and Privacy, Integrity, Usability, Integration, Compliance, Availability and Roles and Responsibilities. DQ is a mandatory part of the overall Data Governance Strategy, as without it the organization will not be able to successfully manage and govern its most strategic asset: its data. Therefore this chapter will focus on the important issue of DQ.

One of the issues with DQ is that organizations are often unclear about who is ultimately responsible for its management. A survey of a group of senior managers in an organization asked, "Who should be responsible for Data Quality in your organization?" The following options were presented to them:

- Board of Directors
- Corporate Executives
- Business unit heads and managers
- Front-line workers
- IT department/Data Warehousing team
- Cross-functional team
- Data Quality analysts/Data stewards
- Others
- No one

The results are represented in Figure 6.1 below.

The diverse responses demonstrates that this management team was divided on who is ultimately responsible with the most popular

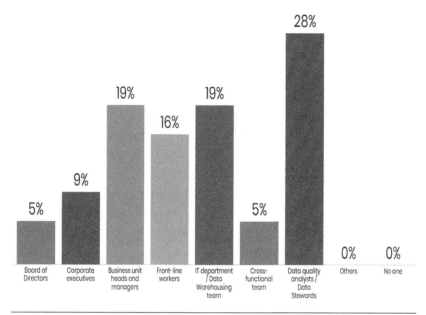

Figure 6.1 Survey of responsibilities for data quality.

choice being the DQ Analysts and Data Stewards at 28%. However, TDWI, an educational and research company for BI and data warehousing states the following:

> To succeed, a data quality program must be initiated by the CEO, overseen by the board of directors, and managed by a chief data quality office or senior-level business managers in each area of the business.[1]

The lack of clarity in terms of responsibility may arise because many business leaders do not understand the critical role the organization's DQ plays in their strategy formulation and how it can affect the strategy execution. Making strategic decisions based on poor quality data can have severe financial and credibility implications.

To overcome this lack of clarity about responsibility PwC provides the following advice:

> Define a Data Strategy and link it to the business and risk strategy such that it leads to Commitment from Senior Management and other stakeholders for implementing a central Data Management strategy; a consistent basis for solutions which support business goals.[2]

---

[1] http://download.101com.com/pub/tdwi/Files/DQReport.pdf.
[2] https://pwc.fr/fr/assets/files/pdf/2016/05/pwc_a4_data_governance_results.pdf.

As organizations seek to develop and leverage core Information Assets and BI capabilities as key enablers of their strategic ambitions, the importance of DQ emerges as a recurrent issue and is perceived by business users as a constraint on the efficiency and effectiveness of various data-driven analytics initiatives and decision-making processes. Experts agree that data needs to be managed like a business critical issue and this requires an enterprise-wide Data Management strategy.

The Information Management (IM) Maturity Assessment conducted as the first step of AIMS-BI identifies gaps in DQ management functions and Data Governance practices. These may include, for example, a lack of DQ metrics, data stewardship, data standardization, metadata management, and profiling and measurement. An example of the IM assessment of the DQ Management functions is shown in Figure 6.2.

The assessment shows a detailed breakdown of some of the specific DQ and Governance issues that organizations face. While many organizations may recognize that they have DQ issues, they may not be clear about the specific nature of these issues. The example assessment below identifies a number of areas in which the organization is particularly weak, including Data Stewardship, Data Standardization, Profiling Measurement.

Organizations are recognizing significant business challenges and opportunity costs that arise as a result of data issues, including ineffective data use; Data Governance focused only on security and

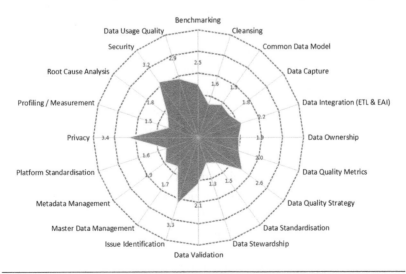

Figure 6.2   IM maturity assessment: data quality management functions.

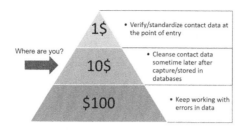

Figure 6.3 Cost pyramid for data quality.

control; a lack of understanding of Data and its impact on business outcomes; reactive, isolated Customer DQ projects and periodic data cleanup initiatives to improve DQ.

Some organizations have invested significantly in comprehensive cleanup exercises, for example, to confirm/update customer's contact information. While these cleanup efforts may yield measurable DQ improvements, these improvements are often short-term. Without the systematic use of specific tools and processes for measuring (profiling) the quality of data assets as a means of monitoring and maintaining progressive DQ improvements, the same errors will reoccur.

The cost pyramid for DQ shown in Figure 6.3 is often used to illustrate the cost impact of different approaches to DQ. It highlights the comparative cost implications of addressing DQ issues at source versus the consequences of cleaning data after capture or working with erroneous data. It clearly demonstrates the importance of a systematic approach to addressing DQ issues early in the process.

Data Quality Management Process

A DQ management process, such as that outlined in Figure 6.4, provides an organization with a set of suggested stages and activities that should be followed if the organization is to treat DQ with the strategic importance that it deserves.

The stages of the DQ Management process, as well as the activities for each of these stages, described in detail below:

Stage 1: Defining Data Standards Quality Metrics

The first stage of the process involves the definitions of data standards and quality metrics. It requires the engagement of key stakeholders

Data Standards Definition / Quality Metrics	Data Quality Assessment	Data Maintenance / Stewardship	Data life-cycle Process Review
• Data standards, Quality metrics & Business rule • Metadata repository (in-scope Customer Data)	• Systematic Data Profiling & Quality Assessment • Data Quality Reports / Visualization Dashboard • Baseline data quality to monitor / track changes in state of data quality over time	• Empower Data stewards to access/view Data Quality metrics • Views / Process for identifying and remediating data quality issues • Batch cleansing mechanisms	• Map / Analyse existing Data Life Cycle • Determine root-cause of Quality Issues • Propose Revised Life Cycle / process adjustments to sustain Data Quality

Figure 6.4   Data quality management process.

within the organization through an established *Data Management Group.*

The output of the data standards development process is a data standards catalog for the data set. The catalog is intended to provide a comprehensive listing of the data items that must be maintained/governed across various systems, according to the agreed standards. The data standards should be specified in a business rather than technical language. Additionally, Data Standards development is seen as an evolutionary process. It is expected that the standards will be reviewed and updated. The composition, size and type of data entities may change due to changes in business requirements and technology. Hence, the standards outlined in the catalog must be subject to change management and version control.

Developing the standards requires a review of existing data entities, formats and validation rules. The standard should be assessed against known Compliance data requirements and data issues and should be defined to ensure that known quality gaps are addressed. A sample data standard definition template is outlined in Table 6.1.

DQ is a multidimensional concept and therefore if an organization is to tackle their quality challenges, the important dimensions of that quality must first be identified. The proposed dimensions should be discussed and agreed on by the *Data Management Group.* Example DQ dimensions and their classification as either objective or subjective are described in Table 6.2.

For each of the data standards the specific objective/subjective DQ indicators which apply to the data element are defined. An example of

Table 6.1 Data Standard Definition Template

METADATA	VALUE
Data Item (DI) name	The full name of the data element
DI description	A simple but unambiguous definition of the data element
DI type	Either string, integer, date/time
Data steward	The role who maintains this data element
Date published	The date this version was published as a data standard <YYYY/MM/DD>
Is part of	The parent element of the data items
Syntax	The required format of the data from the business perspective. This will include the minimum and maximum number of characters, if appropriate, and the structure of the data type or item e.g. National ID business format is NN-NNN-NNN where each N represents a digit from 0 to 9
Validation	Generic for types and specific for items. The validation rules to be applied for acceptance of data
Values	List of the acceptable values (e.g. male, female)
Default value	For any list of values, the default value to be used unless otherwise stated
Verification	Steps taken to establish the correctness of the data type or item
Comments	Additional notes
Data quality dimensions and minimum quality standards	The specific objective/subjective data quality indicators which apply to the data element (e.g. validity, completeness, usability), the metric relevant to each quality indicator and minimum measurement value

one such data item standard (First Name of the Customer) is shown in Table 6.3.

The data standards defined in the catalog must have stakeholder buy-in, therefore they must be signed-off by the members of the *Data Management Group.* It is important to note that different stakeholders may have different notions of acceptable quality standards. For instance, 100% completeness of customer contact information is seen as a required standard by the Compliance group, due to KYC (Know-Your-Customer) Compliance obligations, while the Marketing/Sales department may perceive a 75% completeness as an acceptable standard for effective customer targeting.

Stage 2: Data Quality Assessment

The process of DQ assessment involves systematic data profiling and quality assessment and the generation of DQ reports and visualization dashboards. This process requires that, the tables that have the primary

Table 6.2   Data Quality Dimensions

DIMENSIONS OF DATA QUALITY	DESCRIPTION
Accuracy	The degree to which data correctly reflects the real-world object being described
Validity	The degree to which the data conforms to a standard and business rules
Completeness	The extent to which data is not missing and is of sufficient depth and breadth. The data can be missing at multiple levels: • population – percentage of population represented • schema – attributes/tables missing • data value – missing field values
Consistency	The degree to which the data that exists in multiple locations is similarly represented and/or structured
Integrity	The degree to which data conforms to data relationship rules • Referential integrity • Uniqueness of primary key • Cardinality
Currency	The degree to which data reflects the real-world concept that it represents
Accessibility	The extent to which data is available or easily and quickly retrievable
Uniqueness	The degree to which each data record is unique
Usability	The extent to which business process(es) and/or individuals understand and are able to use this data
Relevancy	The extent to which the data is applicable to one or more business process(es) or decision(s)
Believability	The extent to which data is deemed credible by those using it

Table 6.3   <Salary> Data Standard

ATTRIBUTE	VALUE		
Data Item (DI) name	Salary		
DI description	Represents an employee's salary		
DI type (e.g. string, numeric)	Numeric		
Data steward	HR manager		
Date published	2010/04/03		
Is part of	Employee profile		
Syntax	Minimum X, maximum X numeric value		
Validation	1. No dollar sign 2. No commas		
Values	None		
Default value	Based on job title		
Verification	Should be the person's gross monthly salary		
Comments	All employees must have a salary		
Data quality dimension, metrics and minimum quality standards	DIMENSION	METRIC	MINIMUM STANDARD
	Currency	Binary value (0, 1) based on checks against job description	1 – salary must be within a given range for the job title

source of data under consideration should be identified and used for the DQ assessment phase. A good starting point, in terms of which fields in the tables to use for the profiling, is the unique identifier key (e.g. Customer_ID in a Customer table or Employee_ID in an Employee table). The quality of the unique identifier field is critical to the success of many of the analytics Proof of Concepts as it is often the common field used to join the tables needed for the analytics from across multiple systems. Errors, inconsistencies and missing values in these unique identifier fields will severely limit the results (i.e. number of rows) realized by joining this table with others and thus can significantly reduce the size of the data set to which the analytics will be applied.

The Data Profiling activity conducts an assessment of actual data and data structures and helps to identify DQ issues at the individual attribute level, at the table level, and between tables. Profiling also captures metadata as a by-product of the process.

Two examples of types of profiling analyses that should be carried out on the tables are column profiling and table profiling:

1. Column Profiling involves describing and analyzing the data found in each single column/field of a data table. For example, assume an organization wants to ensure that it can contact its customers and therefore decides to focus on the data relating to "Right Party Contact", Table 6.4 shows the profile for key contact fields in a possible set from aggregated tables. While the column analysis should be performed across all the columns

Table 6.4 Example Profile of Contact Data

VARIABLE	ROWS	FILLED (%)	MISSING (%)	UNIQUE (%)
First name	69,884	100.00	0.00	26.44
Last name	69,884	100.00	0.00	18.34
Address line 1	69,818	99.91	0.09	60.33
Address line 2	56,519	80.88	19.12	27.95
Country of residency	69,664	99.69	0.31	0.05
Nationality	69,664	99.69	0.31	0.16
Branch	69,884	100.00	0.00	0.06
Primary email address	34,227	48.98	51.02	97.93
Primary contact	52,736	75.46	24.54	97.43
Secondary contact	41,974	60.06	39.94	59.53
Customer_TRN	68,630	98.21	1.79	99.83
ID type	69,884	100.00	0.00	0.01

in the table, of special interest are those columns that facilitate "Right Party Contact". It can be seen in the example table below that approximately 75% of primary contact numbers are filled, while email address is just under 50% populated. This gives the organization a good feel of how *contactable* their customers are.

2. Table Profiling involves analyzing data across the rows of a single table to establish dependencies between attributes within the table. For example, Table Profiling can be used to investigate the validity/uniqueness, format accuracy and completeness of the Customer_TRN (a Tax Registration Number which is a unique nine-digit identification number assigned to each individual tax payer, business enterprise or organization by way of an automated system) field of a data set, given its likely importance to the effectiveness of customer analytics initiatives that can span systems and subsidiaries. Figure 6.5 shows as an example of some possible results of profiling the results of the Customer_TRN field. Although this field is expected to be the customer's TRN number which should conform to the specific format (nine digits), the profiling analysis shows multiple formats of the values in the table – most prevalent being a numeric value of length 9, a numeric value of length 7, a value starting with an alpha character followed by seven digits, a numeric value of length 6, as well as a number value of length 9 separated by "–". Additionally, this

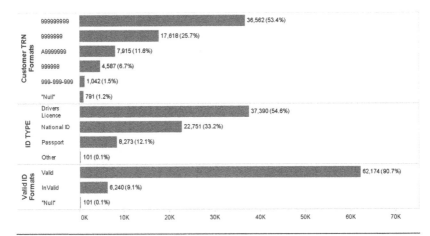

Figure 6.5   Example: profiling Customer_TRN with ID type.

field had a number of null and duplicate values which should never be the case if this is the primary key of the table. If this is to be the field that will be used to join other tables, which is highly likely if it is the key, then the NULL and duplicate values can lead to inconsistencies and inaccuracies. The attributes that are to be used in the analytics PoCs should always be profiled before being included, as poor quality data will lead to poor quality results.

The number of distinctly different formats for the Customer_TRN value would seem puzzling and erroneous, however, it is possible that other unique IDs (for example driver's licence, passport or national ID numbers) were also captured in the field. The existence of metadata would have made this data understanding process less time consuming. Subsequently adding the field ID_Type to the analysis allowed the profiling to identify the number of different ID_Types contained in the field Customer_TRN (see Figure 6.5). Validating the format of the Customer_TRN field against the ID_Type using Regular Expression analysis indicated that 91% of the formats were valid.

Such a variety of personal IDs used as the unique identifiers of customers can become quite confusing in the absence of proper metadata standards. This variety will confound efforts to join the data to other data sources that may have different unique identifier types, adversely impacting the effectiveness of enterprise-level Analytics.

This discussion highlights the importance of using data profiling as an initial step in the data preparation activities associated with analytics initiatives in order to fully understand the contents, interpretation and use of the variables being included in the analytics, as inaccurate or misinterpreted data will lead to inaccurate results and flawed strategic decision-making.

Stage 3: Data Maintenance/Stewardship

The third stage of the DQ management process, data maintenance/ stewardship, includes batch data cleaning efforts to address quality issues detected during DQ assessment. More importantly, a critical aspect of sustainable DQ is to identify and empower data stewards to help formulate and oversee adherence to DQ standards and policies. This data stewardship role requires both technical and business inputs as the steward must also ensure that standardized data element definitions and formats are being adhered to and that the metadata is being maintained. Stewards also manage the process of identifying and resolving any emerging DQ issues and oversee periodic batch cleansing activities.

DQ dashboards have increasingly become an effective means of creating the essential visibility needed to facilitate monitoring and reporting on DQ metrics and compliance over time. They provide an important tool for enabling and empowering data stewards to assess the state of DQ, and address root cause process issues within their designated jurisdiction. Key to the design of DQ dashboards is understanding and identifying the key quality indicators (KQI) that the organization needs to track, monitor and manage. Figure 6.6 displays an example DQ dashboard that emphasizes the quality status for a key "Unique Identifier" and "Rights Party Contact" fields that are essential for maintaining effective customer analytics and contact management. As highlighted on the "Dashboard", an organization would be able to establish a baseline, then monitor progressive improvements in these key data items over time, based on various DQ interventions. These quality attributes can be stored as part of an enterprise metadata repository, in order to facilitate historical trending of DQ improvements as part of a comprehensive data governance/information life-cycle management process.

For DQ dashboards to be most effective, especially for Executives, it is useful to combine the data profiling information from individual variables into aggregate business metrics. For example, in the prototype dashboard in Figure 6.6, a simple business metric has been created called **RPC_ndx,** which provides a quantitative indicator of the organization's "ability to contact" its customers. The metric is computed from *Name, Address, Telephone#, Email* as follows:

$$\textbf{RPC\_ndx:} \left[\text{Name} * 1 + (\text{Address}) * 1 + \text{Telephone} * 1 + \text{Email} * 2 \right] / 5$$

In this case, it has been determined that having valid email contact information for a customer contributes twice as much value to this business metric than any other contact attribute.

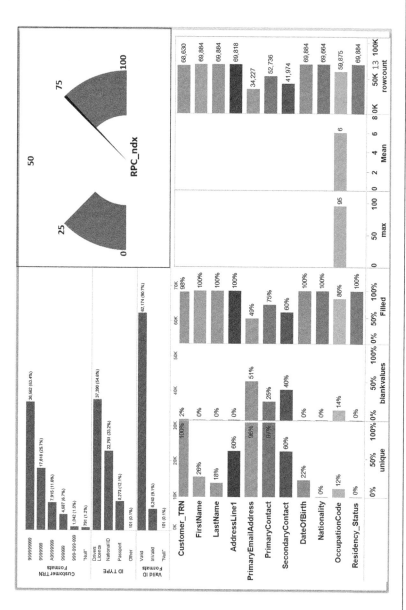

Figure 6.6 Example: data quality dashboard.

Stage 4: Data Life-Cycle Process Review

The final stage of the DQ management process facilitates root cause analysis and systematic data life-cycle process improvements to minimize the recurring incidence of new quality issues and the need for extensive periodic batch cleaning exercises. It begins with the mapping of the existing data life cycle which provides stakeholders with a better understanding of the critical data points from its initial creation, including integration across systems, access, retention and eventual disposal. For example, it will show where the various data items are captured and by which roles, how the data items are being used and the possible points at which the quality can be compromised. A critical objective of establishing this mapping is to provide input for the root cause analysis. As previously pointed out, it is inefficient for an organization to undergo extensive periodic batch cleaning exercises without addressing the root cause of the problem as these problems, if not addressed at the source, will reoccur. Many organizations do not have a systematic approach to root cause analysis for information/ DQ issues and, if this is the case, it will be reflected in the results from the IM maturity assessment.

Once the existing process is mapped and the root cause analysis performed, the appropriate revisions to problematic business processes can be identified and addressed. In this more systematic approach to data governance, the emphasis is on modifying people's attitudes and improving processes and the strategy is focused on establishing effective DQ policies and control processes based on DQ standards and rules. Supporting mechanisms include automating the monitoring and reporting of DQ metrics and communicating knowledge about the value of the data and the importance of DQ across the business.

One common and useful DQ PoC that organizations should consider as they build out their portfolios is the mapping of the data life-cycle processes around key customer contact data.

Conclusion

DQ is a recurrent issue across organizations, and is perceived by business users as a constraint on the efficiency and effectiveness of various data-driven analytics initiatives and decision-making processes.

The effectiveness of the analytics PoCs is often limited by several aspects of DQ. Other than the obvious issue of accuracy (i.e. degree to which data values are correct), inconsistent data formats, missing values, same field names with different meanings from different data sources, identification of logical relatedness between specific data instances based on values are all common issues encountered across organizations that highlight the need for a more systematic approach to DQ. A DQ PoC is important as it demonstrates the benefits of a systematic approach to DQ standards definition and DQ measurement. The use of a DQ Dashboard can help empower data stewards in formulating and overseeing adherence to DQ standards and policies across the business. The following specific recommendations/observations are highlighted:

- Establishing a formal Data Governance framework, both in terms of the core discipline of DQ Management as well as institutional approaches to Data Stewardship, should be an immediate priority for organizations that do not currently have this in place.
- Formal Metadata Management and Data Standards Catalogs are critical for the efficient development of PoCs and subsequent analytics initiatives. The absence of metadata can lead to reduced throughput in data preparation activities, misinterpretation of data items and inaccurate interpretation of analytics results. The Data Standards catalog will include all of the primary Data Sources and key fields and the Metadata catalog will provide a centralized, searchable electronic repository of data assets
- It is recommended that organizations invest in an Enterprise data integration platform, e.g. Talend, that can be employed in the Data Integration/DQ PoCs. Such platforms enable more systematic approaches to the logical and physical definition and standardization of data across the enterprise, and enhance the efficiency of the definition, storage, movement and delivery of data to business analysts and decision-makers.
- Special emphasis should be placed on monitoring, tracking and managing the quality of a relatively small set of critical data items for integration purposes, using DQ Dashboards and Stewards. Null data values, missing data and inconsistent data,

especially in the primary key fields, (e.g. Customer ID) can significantly impact the analytic benefits/value of integration.

- Related to the previous point, Master Data Management for key data entities, for example Customer, will become important for managing data consistency across the subsidiaries and systems throughout the organization.

- Effective analytics are dependent on the availability and currency of data over time. If the data values are not being updated, the analytics will reflect inaccurate trends and will greatly impact the decision-making. For example, the customer's home address, marital status and occupation may emerge as significant predictor fields but if they are not current and do not reflect how they have changed over time, erroneous inferences could be drawn. Therefore, part of the data governance mechanism should seek to maintain the currency of key data items.

- The primary rationale for BI should be to realize maximum returns from data assets. Returns may take the form of increases in operational efficiency, employee productivity, time to market, sales and revenue, as well as mitigating costs which may be realized as process failures, opportunity costs, scrap and rework costs, and the failure to sense and act on business opportunities. Developing economic models for the value of information and opportunity costs of DQ can be demonstrated in a PoC but should be extended and institutionalized to provide the organization with systemic approaches to measurement, ranking and quantification of data/information value creation activities.

- Establish a formal DQ Management process, facilitated by an Enterprise DQ Platform that integrates all of the requisite functions, including profiling, cleansing, standardization and DQ Dashboard functions to monitor DQ metrics and support data governance initiatives.

- Institutionalizing Data Stewardship includes defining the necessary roles, procedures and support mechanisms and identifying and empowering Data Stewards to help formulate and oversee adherence to DQ standards and policies.

7

DATA INTEGRATION

Managing Data Sources for Agility

> It's difficult to imagine the power that you're going to have when so many different sorts of data are available.

Tim Berners-Lee

Introduction

As organizations seek to increase their use of analytics, their business analysts and decision-makers require access to additional, non-conventional sources of data, in a timely manner, in order to experiment, prototype and evaluate various analytics initiatives. Achieving this timely access to data requires greater *agility* in data integration and the capability and tools to rapidly access and integrate data from multiple heterogeneous sources. This integration will provide decision-makers with the flexibility to explore, and prototype various Business Intelligence (BI) initiatives, and better control the scope, cost and timeline of their implementation/evaluation.

The emerging discipline(s) of "Data Virtualization" and "Data as a Service" together with a new breed of Open Source platforms present alternative, lower cost approaches to the traditional ETL/Data Warehousing applications for Data Integration within the enterprise. They provide a range of functions (e.g. Federation, Transformation, Profiling, Cleaning, Interface handling) and Data Delivery Services (e.g. model-driven Metadata services, Data access Web service APIs),[1] to enable agile approaches to BI. These approaches to low-cost, agile integration are critical for strategic BI adoption by Small and Medium-Sized Enterprises (SMEs).

---

[1] Application Program Interface.

This chapter will evaluate the approaches, challenges and benefits of data integration, demonstrate the emerging "data virtualization" techniques and highlight the importance of (meta)data standardization to enhance this process. It provides further discussions of how agility is achieved in the data integration step of AIMS-BI.

Opportunities through Data Integration

As organizations seek to harness more value from their data assets, they recognize the importance of integrating existing, disparate, heterogeneous sources of data for improved decision-making. In organizations, data often exists in silos and needs to be connected for its full potential to be realized. Figure 7.1 shows various types of customer data that may exist in different locations and which, if integrated, can provide a 360° view of the customer. For example, a financial institution may have customers' demographics in one data source and details of their transactions, such as daily/monthly withdrawals/deposits or financial instruments purchased, in another data store. If the customer has a debit/credit card, their behavioral data is captured in the point of sales transactional database while their queries and complaints may be stored in a customer center database. Integrating

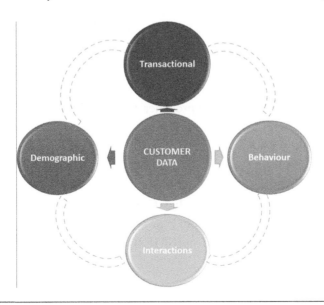

Figure 7.1   Connecting customer data.

these disparate sources of customer data provides a core platform for enhanced analytics.

The traditional approach of building a Data Warehouse for integration purposes is now being seen as too rigid and too resource intensive for some types of organizations. For example, SMEs may not have the human and capital resources that are associated with the development of a Data Warehouse. With this in mind, the main objectives of this chapter are first to explore the various integration techniques and then to demonstrate non-traditional opportunities that may be suited to SMEs. These opportunities include:

1. Improving business analysts' productivity/efficiency by increasing their access to various internal/external data sets through increased self-service data access and improved turnaround on data service requests. More specifically by:
   a. Enabling efficient access to data across multiple heterogeneous data stores;
   b. Enabling on-demand access for analysts to data that is not already in an intermediary data store;
   c. Increasing visibility (publishing) of available intermediary stores and facilitating wider, controlled access to analysts;
   d. Facilitating the creation of *data mashups*[2] which can be published to other analysts.
2. Demonstrating the effective use of new information infrastructure solutions/tools to support key information management functions and bolster business analytics capabilities.

Key Deliverables from Realizing Integration Opportunities

The opportunities above, if met, will lead to a number of deliverables that the organization can adopt for their strategic BI roadmap. These deliverables include:

1. The identification and installation of the appropriate information infrastructure/tool that can be used to (i) demonstrate to key stakeholders the key capabilities listed from 1a. to 1d. above and (ii) make required data available for any analytics

---

[2] Data mashups integrate heterogeneous data from multiple data sources.

PoCs the organization selects based on Steps 2 and 3 of AIMS-BI (i.e. BI opportunity portfolio development and prioritization).

2. Data integration technology selection and implementation guidelines documentation published for the organization's technical team.
3. Recommendations for possible continued use of the open source tools (or other existing tools) as part of the BI roadmap.

As a part of the integration process, an important Key Performance Indicator (KPI) to be considered is to *improve data usage quality*. Data usage quality measures the extent to which users trust, have ready access to, and make effective use of organizational data.

Common Approach to Data Integration

For many organizations, their primary data assets reside in several enterprise systems. For example, a financial institution may have some data in the core banking application, some with the credit card application, some with loan application and some with the Customer Relationship Management System. These systems may be using, for example, Oracle or SQL Server database platforms. It is likely that, in the existing setup, various mechanisms (e.g. Redpoint, Microsoft SQL Server Integration Services (SSIS) and native SQL queries) are being used to extract data from the sources to serve business analytics and decision-support requirements. In addition, end-user departments may be using a variety of their own customized tools (e.g. Excel spreadsheets) to access, retrieve, clean and analyze data relevant to their needs. However, this practice often constrains the flexibility and timeliness with which the organization can respond to new requests for access to, and integration of, data from multiple heterogeneous sources (internal and external).

Possible Integration Approaches

There are a number of approaches to data integration that have been classified in various ways. One possible way to view this is to consider two broad classes that are distinguishable based on whether the data is physically integrated or logically integrated:

Table 7.1 Data Integration Techniques

CLASS	EXAMPLE TECHNIQUE	DESCRIPTION
Physical integration	Data consolidation	Brings data together from several separate systems into one physical data store
	Data warehouse (DW)/data mart	Data from heterogeneous sources is integrated in advance and stored in a DW
Virtual integration "virtualization"	Data federation	Uses a virtual database and creates a common data model for heterogeneous data from different systems
	Enterprise Service Bus (ESB)	Used to develop a layer of services that allow access to data that remain at their source

   i. Physical integration – this involves the integration of the data from several sources into a new physical data source whether termed a database, data repository or a data warehouse (DW).

  ii. Logical/Virtual integration – this involves the integration of data without creating another physical data store, but rather by providing an interface to a unified view of the data that remains in these disparate data stores. Through this interface, the technical aspects of the stored data are *hidden* from the data consumer, i.e. to the consumer it is as if they are accessing data from a single data source. There are various ways in which both the physical and logical integration approaches can be realized, some examples of each are identified in Table 7.1 and are described further in the following section.

Examples of Data Integration Techniques

Physical Integration

  a. Data Consolidation – Data consolidation physically brings data together from several separate systems thus creating a version of the consolidated data in one data store. The Extraction, Transformation and Loading (ETL) technology supports data consolidation. The ETL process is responsible for pulling the data from the disparate sources, transforming it into an understandable format and loading it into another database or DW.

  b. Data Warehouse (DW) – A DW is a physical repository of historical, enterprise-wide data, cleaned to ensure that it is of a high quality, obtained from internal and possibly external sources. The data loaded into the warehouse is perceived as being critically important for strategic decision-making. The data is organized and structured to ensure that it can be accessed efficiently for the strategic type of analysis for which the warehouse is designed. The building of this DW will include the consolidation of data.

Virtual Integration

1. Data Federation: A form of data virtualization which utilizes a virtual database to create a common data model for heterogeneous data from disparate systems. The data is viewable from a single point of access which can be implemented using technologies such as Enterprise Information Integration (EII).

2. Enterprise Service Bus (ESB): The ESB is an abstraction layer which can be used to develop a set of services that allow access to the data without the users knowing the details of where and how it is stored. This approach does not require a common data model as the data federation approach does, rather, each source provides a service by exposing its features and communicating with other services offered by other sources. The application invoking the services does not need to know where the data is stored, what the original source interface is and how the data is stored at the source; it will only see an Application Programming Interface (API) such as SOAP (Simple Object Access Protocol) or REST (Representational State Transfer) which is the mechanism used for sources to expose their services.

Physical vs. Virtual Integration

There are several factors to be considered when choosing between physical and virtual integration. The physical integration approach is considered to be *update-driven* as the data from the disparate sources is loaded in advance and stored in the destination source for direct querying and analysis. Additionally, when the source changes, the data in the destination is refreshed periodically to reflect these changes. On the other hand, the logical integration approach is viewed as *query-driven* as the data is retrieved from the source on an *as need be* basis. Each time a query is posed it is translated to queries on the source where the relevant data is stored.

There are a number of advantages to the physical approach that have made, for example, the DW Warehouse approach a popular choice for integration. These benefits include the ability to design the DW to ensure efficient query performance for strategic type queries. However, because the data sources are designed to ensure the efficiency of transactional type (e.g. SQL) queries, this design is not suitable for the analytic type queries. Keeping the two sets of stores separate allows each to be designed to optimize the types of queries that are being posed on them. This means that the local transactional type processing at the source will be unaffected by the demands being placed on it by the strategic queries and that the integrated source can be designed for the specific needs of strategic analytical queries (e.g. data summarization). Additionally, if the source is down for any reason, the data is still available at the integrated source (i.e. there is some data replication). Finally, when loading data into a physical store it is possible to include additional data including data from external sources which can provide added value when integrated with the already existing internal data and historical data which is not typically kept at the source given that transactional query processing largely involves the updating of the existing data. Updating the data means that the historical perspective of how the data changes over time is not typically captured at the source. In the case of the DW approach, as new data is loaded into the warehouse, rather than updating the existing data, it is appended to the existing data thereby facilitating the historical perspective needed for BI and analytics. The warehouse design facilitates the storing of aggregated and summarized data which is what is primarily used for BI and analytics; thus precomputing and storing the aggregated data improves the efficiency of the analytics. Finally, another major benefit of the physical integration approach is that in the development of the destination source, especially in the case of the DW, the data that is loaded would have gone through an extensive cleaning process to remove data quality issues and a transformation process to ensure the data is in a format suited for analytics. This means that the destination source is a clean, integrated, transformed, summarized data set that is suited for analytics purposes. In the case of logical integration, the data is extracted from the source and can have quality issues which must be addressed on a need-be basis with a logical approach and can become difficult to manage.

However, even with all the benefits the physical approach offers, there are some major drawbacks which make it infeasible for certain types of organizations. The most obvious is that there is an additional physical store of data and so the storage needs increase significantly especially as the integrated data store includes historical data. Another issue with the physical approach is that the data in the integrated source may not always be reflective of the data at the source. This is due to the fact that the Extraction Transformation and Load (ETL) process is done periodically and therefore the integrated data source does not always have the most up-to-date data. In the logical approach this issue would not arise, data that is needed for processing a query is retrieved from the source at the time requested. The DW approach is also seen as complex, rigid, costly, time consuming and resource intensive and there are many cases of failed DW initiatives even with significant initial investments. Therefore, the physical integration option is seen as impractical for some organizations, particularly Small and Medium-Sized Enterprises (SMEs). Thus, lower cost, less resource intensive, more agile approaches have been sought which gave rise to a number of alternative approaches, such as logical data integration.

Organizations, such as SMEs, that are looking to these alternatives as options can also consider the Open Source solutions that are now available. These Open Source solutions require a smaller initial investment of resources and are extremely beneficial for PoCs that can be used to demonstrate the importance and power of data integration as they provide a quick turnaround without a significant cost.

Selecting a Data Integration Approach

Given the number of approaches that are now available for Data Integration, an organization needs to be deliberate in determining which option is most appropriate for its needs. An example of the functionality for Data Integration is illustrated in Figure 7.2.

This target functionality can be achieved by:

1. Evaluating available Open Source platforms using an established Open Source Maturity Model to select an appropriate Data Integration technology solution.

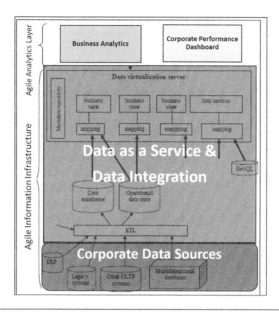

Figure 7.2 A high level architecture of an agile BI system.

2. Evaluating the performance of the Data Integration platform connectivity to core organizational data sources to determine feasible configuration options ranging from traditional Extract, Transform and Load (ETL) to virtual integration.

3. Evaluating various data management functionalities, such as:

   a. Data Integration: *Federation, Interface handling, Transformation, Profiling.*

   b. Data services delivery: *Model-driven Metadata services, Web service APIs for data access, Master Data Management.*

There are a number of options for Open Source tools (e.g. Talend and Pentaho) that can be evaluated. The next section provides a summary of some of the features that are seen in these platforms. The features are classified based on the following themes and are displayed in Table 7.2.

- Data Integration – Ability to connect data from multiple sources.
- Data Management – Understanding, organizing and storing data.
- Data Delivery – Flexible delivery of data.
- Technical Infrastructure – Servers, networks and software.

Table 7.2   Themes and Features for Managing Data

CATEGORY/THEME	PRODUCT FEATURE
Data integration	Data integration: connect to multiple data sources (traditional, Big Data & NoSQL)
Data integration	Data integration: support Extract Transform and Load (ETL), data federation
Data integration	Dynamic data modelling & integration: easy-to-use, graphical, drag-and-drop tools to build processes and transformations
Data management	Metadata management: model-driven metadata services & directory search using a single metadata repository
Data management	Data quality/data profiling: tools that profile and cleanse data, parse and standardize data, and match, merge, etc.
Data management	Master data management: create a unified view of information and manage that master view over time
Data delivery	Data as a service: deliver data to consumers via Web service APIs RESTful/SOAP)
Data delivery	Reports and dashboards: pre-built and customizable reports/ dashboards that show key data quality metrics
Technical infrastructure	Multi-platform runtime support: ability to deploy to Linux-based and windows systems, cloud and virtualization environments
Technical infrastructure	Web-based monitoring: ability to monitor resources and deployments from any browser

Recommendations for SMEs

The design and implementation of the classic data warehouse architecture that underpins many BI Systems can be technically and financially daunting for organizations without the requisite technical resources. Smaller organizations in particular are often challenged by the complexity and resource requirements of traditional BI solutions. New data integration techniques combined with cloud services provide more flexible and more agile options for SMEs.

The data-as-a-service platforms improve the efficiency of accessing existing intermediary stores as the web services allow for on-demand access to data, thereby eliminating the need for the input of an IT data specialist. For example, a web service can expose the *data in a data store* so that an analyst can access it directly. Additionally, the tools for data integration enable analysts to create data mashups (i.e. integration of two or more data sets in a single graphical interface) themselves, without relying on a data specialist. This means that the existing data can be used more flexibly, thus increasing its use.

Using a tool to connect to a diverse set of sources and that allows easy extraction and manipulation of data directly from the core data sources increases an organization's ability to be agile. This ability to extract data, using a simple web service, will greatly improve the efficiency of the analysts as they can now access data as needed, rather than having to wait until it is moved to an intermediary store.

Conclusion

Data integration is a fundamental issue for any organization considering investing in BI initiatives. While the importance of this step is recognized, the actual commitment, in terms of time and resources, required to carry it out successfully is often underestimated. The success of data integration is highly dependent on data quality and governance. Any issues related to poor quality and governance, will reduce the integration opportunities and increase the cost and resources needed to perform it. The application of the IM assessment as the first step of the methodology will provide some important insights in terms of the readiness of the organization for effective data integration.

Diverse options and the tools available for data integration allow SMEs and similar organizations that were previously disadvantaged due to the investments required by traditional methods, to now consider integration as an important part of their portfolio as they adopt BI. The newer opportunities also provide a more flexible and agile approach to integration which is important given the environment in which these organizations are operating.

PART III
A BLUEPRINT FOR ACTION

This section describes the development of the Business Intelligence (BI) roadmap, which identifies the activities that organizations should focus on if they hope to become serious contenders in the strategic BI space.

Chapter 8 describes how the outcomes and findings from the preceding steps of AIMS-BI are integrated into a strategic BI roadmap. This strategic BI roadmap reflects a balanced portfolio of BI initiatives and a coherent implementation sequence, and provides a sound basis for ensuring that BI initiatives are aligned to organizational strategic priorities.

Chapter 9 addresses the systematic means by which organizations realize value from their information assets and BI initiatives. It begins by emphasizing the need for them to estimate the business value that is embedded in their data assets. Once organizations ascribe a business value to their data assets, it becomes easier for executive management to appreciate and elevate the strategic importance of managing these assets. Thereafter, Benefits Realization Management (BRM) can be employed as a collective set of processes, practices, and tools that help the organization to increase the likelihood that benefits are realized from BI and other ICT-enabled initiatives. Finally, in the epilogue, we highlight, based on our experience, some of the factors we consider to be essential for the successful implementation of AIMS-BI in SMEs and those activities which are relevant to the needs of these enterprises but that have not been considered in more traditional BI approaches.

8

DEVELOPING A ROADMAP
FOR STRATEGIC BUSINESS
INTELLIGENCE

If you don't know where you are going, any road will get you there.

Lewis Carroll

Introduction

This chapter describes how the results of the preceding steps of AIMS-BI are integrated into a strategic Business Intelligence (BI) roadmap. Both the IM maturity assessment and the PoCs are integral to the development of the strategic BI roadmap as both identify key areas on which the organization needs to focus and develop capabilities if it is to maximize the benefits of its investment in strategic BI. The preceding steps also ensure that the roadmap developed through AIMS-BI is tailored to each particular organization's strategic BI requirements. Figure 8.1 identifies the various activities of AIMS-BI that inform the strategic BI roadmap.

The roadmap provides a balanced portfolio of BI initiatives; these initiatives include technology and analytics projects, as well as capacity building/training, creating organizational structures/roles and policy initiatives. The initial roadmap sequencing reflects the concurrent need for both developmental and applied initiatives that address critical gaps identified from the IM maturity assessment, while generating early returns from existing or enhanced capabilities.

This strategic BI roadmap reflects a balanced portfolio of BI initiatives and a coherent implementation sequence, and provides a sound basis for ensuring that BI initiatives are aligned to organizational strategic priorities. This chapter highlights the importance of

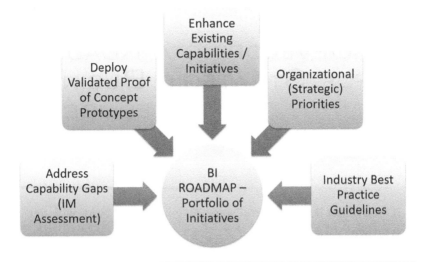

Figure 8.1   Interventions to inform the strategic BI roadmap.

a strategic BI roadmap in placing the organization in a position to secure executive commitment and resources and, in so doing, putting the organization on the path to becoming a serious "Analytics Competitor".

Information Management (IM) Maturity Assessment (Capability Gaps)

The IM maturity assessment report is a key input into the development of the strategic BI roadmap. As described in depth in Chapter 3, the assessment selects six domains across an organization: *People/Organization, Policy, Technology, Compliance, Measurement* and *Process/Practice*, and assesses various functional competencies (e.g. *Data Quality Strategy, Data Ownership, Executive Sponsorship*) within each of these domains. The breadth of the coverage of the IM maturity assessment is representative of the scope of the IM capability required. An example of the results of the assessment are visually represented in Figure 8.2, using the IBM Data Governance Council (IBM-DGC) reference model. This representation has the advantage of highlighting the interconnectedness and path dependencies between the various aspects of IM maturity and the most critical capability gaps to be addressed. For instance, Data Quality Management, Information Lifecycle Management and Information Security and Privacy are the

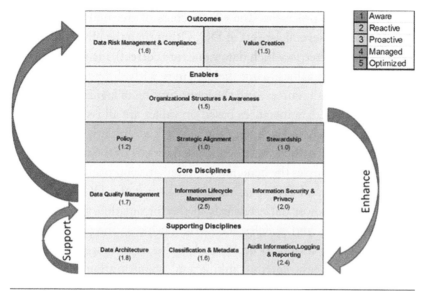

Figure 8.2   Information maturity assessment – IBM-DGC model perspective.

three core disciplines required for organizations to be able to real-ize desirable value outcomes from BI. However, having key enablers, such as Organizational Structures and Awareness, Policy, Strategic Alignment and Stewardship, in place will enhance the effectiveness of the core disciplines. Based on the IM maturity assessment, initiatives are identified and included in the BI roadmap.

Proof of Concept (PoC) Prototypes

The BI (PoCs) prototypes highlight the potential for the application of BI analytics techniques on the significant data resources and assets owned by the organization. The PoCs deliver working prototypes that provide the basis for the accelerated deployment of production appli-cations which, with incremental development effort, could become valuable components of the organizations analytics portfolio.

Data Quality

Data Quality (DQ) emerges as a recurrent issue in many organiza-tions and is perceived by organizations as a constraint on the effi-ciency and effectiveness of various data-driven analytics initiatives and decision-making processes. The effectiveness of the analytics PoCs is often limited by several aspects of DQ. Other than the obvious issue of accuracy (i.e. degree to which data values are correct), inconsistent data formats, missing values, same field names with different meanings from different data sources, and the identification of logical relatedness between specific data instances based on values are all issues that may be encountered when developing the prototypes. Initiatives to address the DQ issues identified must be included as part of the roadmap.

Chapter 6 discusses the benefits of a systematic approach to DQ standards definition and DQ measurement. The use of a DQ Dashboard can help to empower data stewards in the formulation and oversight of DQ standards and policies across the business. The principal DQ and Governance lesson to be learned is the importance of systemic approaches to measurement, ranking and quantification of DQ and asset value, so that the organization can begin to better manage and maximize returns on its data investments. Thus, DQ and Governance is likely to become a critical aspect of the BI roadmap.

Data Integration

The Data Integration stage (see Chapter 7) demonstrates the value of utilizing a specialized data integration platform. Data Integration at the prototype development stage can be performed using open source options (e.g. Open Source community edition of the Talend Open Studio Platform). The use of open source options at this stage allows for rapid development without the need for significant investment in resources. However, when considering a full-blown implementation, a subscription-based Enterprise Platform might be more suitable for the Data Integration needs identified. The organization should consider deploying this option to enable more systematic approaches to the logical and physical definition and standardization of data across the enterprise and the on-demand delivery of data services to a range of information consumers.

Any platform should also support (i) the Data standards Cataloguing (ii) Metadata Management and (iii) DQ Management (Profiling/Dashboard) functionalities identified in Chapter 6 in order to facilitate the formalizing of Data Governance/Stewardship roles, procedures and supporting mechanisms.

Architecture of a Business Intelligence (BI) Roadmap

Gartner emphasizes the complex orchestration of program management, technology, institutional mechanisms and skills required for the strategic use of BI. They also underscore the need for a framework that defines the layers and components that are to be integrated and aligned in order to deliver a more strategic vision and plan for implementing BI, analytics and performance management (PM) initiatives (see Figure 8.3). The Gartner Business Analytics framework,[1] is a high-level framework that provides a practical basis for representing an enterprise BI Roadmap, is used to situate the various BI initiatives derived from applying the AIMS-BI methodology. The BI roadmap will be guided by the following summarized adaptation of Gartner's recommendations on the use of this framework:

- The framework should be used to develop a strategy and an implementation plan, and to highlight key decisions, integration points, gaps, overlaps and biases;
- A portfolio of IM, analytic and decision-making capabilities will be needed to meet the diverse requirements of the organization;

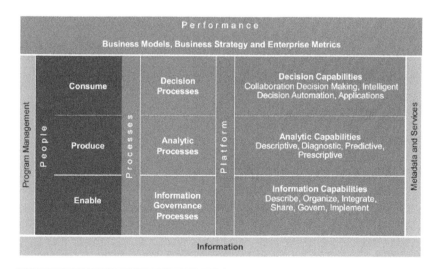

Figure 8.3   The Gartner business analytics framework.

---

[1] https://gartner.com/imagesrv/summits/docs/na/business-intelligence/gartners_business_analytics__219420.pdf.

- Formal Program Management (PM) will be required to balance resources and investments across multiple BI, Analytics and PM initiatives and projects;
- BI initiatives are best suited to iterative development and should be driven by a BI competency center (BICC) that gathers requirements, prioritizes needs and delivers solutions in phases.

The components of the Gartner Framework and their application to an organization's BI roadmap are as follows:

Performance

PM links the strategic goals of the business with the execution of these goals and seeks to align operational activities and processes with an appropriate enterprise metrics framework. The explicit statement of strategic priorities and key performance indicators (KPIs) in the BI Roadmap help to ensure that BI initiatives are aligned to organizational strategic priorities. During Steps 2 and 3 of AIMS-BI the selected PoCs are aligned with the strategic objectives of the organization, as identified by key stakeholders. As well as the explicit statement of strategic priorities and KPIs, an Enterprise Performance Management system/Dashboard is one of the recommended early BI initiatives that should be contained in a BI Roadmap, as it will help executives to measure and track the impact and effectiveness of the BI program as it is rolled out.

People

This layer of the framework addresses BI initiatives that focus on the development and institutionalization of people capabilities and roles based on the task perspectives of *producers*, *consumers* and *enablers*:

Producers – Domain experts/business analysts who analyze data, specify and develop analytic models, produce reports and dashboards, provide insights into business performance and support the decision-making process. Effective data integration and the availability of data self-service platforms make the process of acquiring relevant data easy and efficient and allow *producers* to conduct analytical tasks independently of IT support. The producers need knowledge and expertise across a wide competency spectrum ranging from technical skills associated with modeling and analysis tools to a deep understanding of business issues and their corresponding performance impact, along with good communication skills.

Consumers – Persons within the organization who consume the results and insights of analytics to either make decisions or take actions. Consumers are instrumental in ensuring that the results of analytics are operationalized in the institution; they include operational workers, such as sales representatives who are making the day-to-day decisions within a particular product domain; functional managers making operational and tactical decisions; and senior executives responsible for strategic decision-making. BI initiatives targeting consumers include function-specific performance dashboards and scorecards as well as decision-support applications and tools.

Enablers – The information technology professionals within the organization and external supporting vendors and/or consultants who are responsible for designing, building and maintaining the platforms and systems used by producers and consumers. The IM maturity assessment will help to identify areas in which the organization needs to invest, in terms of the technical platforms and capabilities, in order to more effectively deliver the requisite IM disciplines and services, e.g. *Data Architecture*, *Metadata Management* and *Data Quality Management*. However, the requirements for *enablers* go beyond technology competencies to encompass subject area domain expertise and business communications skills. Among the enablers should be someone with the designated role of Data Steward who is provided with the supporting structures and processes required to establish and maintain data quality accountability across the business. It is unlikely that all these capabilities will reside in a single individual; therefore the organization may need to consider the establishment of a BI Competency Center to consolidate internal core BI expertise and capabilities to be augmented, where necessary, with resources from outside the organization.

Process

The Gartner framework highlights three interconnected groups of processes: *decision processes, analytical processes* and *information governance processes*. The *Information governance processes* enable the *analytical processes* through supporting mechanisms such as data governance, data stewardship, data integration and data quality management which are essential for BI initiatives to be successful. The business impact of the *analytical processes* is realized through effective *decision processes*, which ensure that the outputs of the analytics are deployed to enhance decision-making and business value. Several of the BI initiatives in the roadmap are likely to focus on improved *information governance* and *analytical processes*. A standardized template for specifying analytics initiatives will ensure that key questions are addressed when formulating BI initiatives. This template includes explicitly defining a deployment strategy as part of each analytic initiative as this will enhance the effectiveness of the associated *decision processes*.

Platform

The platform layer integrates the technology required to manage data and information with the tools to build analytical capabilities as well as the technology that improves decision-making capabilities. The information capability layer is foundational and the data integration and data quality PoCs, which in many cases will be identified as mandatory, will inform key BI platform initiatives. Built on top of this layer is the analytical capability layer which includes descriptive, predictive and prescriptive analytics, several of which are identified and evaluated during Steps 2 and 3 of AIMS-BI. Applying the insights and output of BI and analytics will require technology *enablers* to work closely with information *producers* and *consumers* in order to understand and model the business decisions. This end-to-end BI process requires the integration of information capabilities, analytic capabilities and decision capabilities to facilitate acquiring good quality data, performing advanced analytics and enabling the sales teams to target the right customers with the right products.

Example Roadmap – Portfolio of BI Initiatives

An example portfolio of BI initiatives and strategic BI roadmap for a generic financial institution is represented in Figure 8.4. This roadmap, which is derived from applying the steps of AIMS-BI, provides a balanced portfolio of BI initiatives that includes technology and analytics projects, as well as capacity building/training, organizational structures/roles and policy initiatives. Key features of this derived BI roadmap include:

- **Enterprise scope, incremental execution**: The BI portfolio reflects a full spectrum of initiatives that will impact all areas of the organization, including the IT division, from branch operations to the various subsidiaries, and from executive management to line staff. However, it is designed in such a way that its execution can be planned incrementally based on the organization's absorptive capacity for change and without overcommitting financial or human resources.
- **Bootstrap initiatives**: The completed PoC prototypes provide the basis for the accelerated deployment of BI initiatives that can lead to important early wins and demonstrable value in the execution of the roadmap.
- **Development, leverage and application of BI capabilities**: The roadmap provides a mix of development and application initiatives that allows for concurrently addressing critical gaps identified from the IM maturity assessment while generating early returns from existing or enhanced capabilities.
- **Intrinsic Progress Monitoring**: The built-in annual IM maturity assessment provides a systematic means by which the organization measures improvements in its IM and BI capabilities. The Enterprise Performance Management System/Dashboard is likely to be one of the BI initiatives

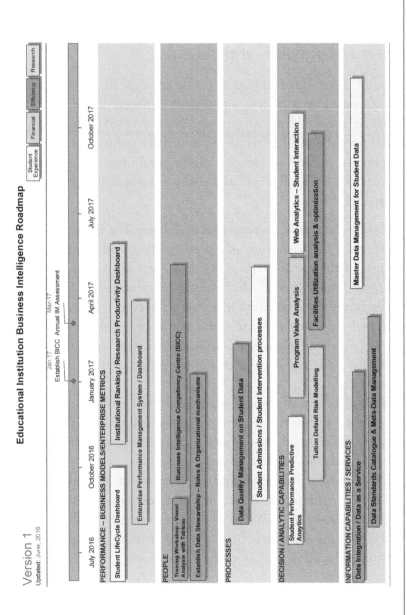

Figure 8.4 Example of a strategic roadmap.

recommended for early implementation based on the BI roadmap. It will help executives to track the realized business impact and effectiveness of the BI program as it is rolled out.

Navigating the BI Roadmap

The organization's strategic BI roadmap (Figure 8.4) is designed as a dynamic portfolio of initiatives that covers an initial timespan (e.g. 18 months) and is amenable to enterprise-level Project Portfolio Management (PPM) best practices. The association of each initiative with the organization's stated strategic priorities allows for the dynamic allocation of financial and human resources in alignment with shifting or emergent business priorities.

The initial roadmap sequencing reflects the concurrent need for both developmental and applied initiatives that address critical gaps identified by the IM maturity assessment, while generating early returns from existing or enhanced capabilities. Based on each annual scheduled maturity assessment, the roadmap can be recalibrated to reflect developmental progress in addressing maturity levels across the dimensions of *People/Organization*, *Policy*, *Technology*, *Compliance*, *Measurement* and *Process/Practice*. It is important that the organization maintains a balanced effort across the five layers reflected in the roadmap until the initial portfolio of initiatives is completed.

The organization's team that is assigned responsibility for the execution of the BI roadmap should undertake a more detailed profiling of each of the individual initiatives in terms of estimated costs and projected benefits, manpower/expertise resource requirements and technology dependencies. This will facilitate more effective PPM and ultimately help the organization to realize an effective BI strategy, develop core BI capabilities, align with any ongoing changes in strategic priorities and optimize its BI investments.

Conclusion

A strategic BI roadmap provides a big picture of where the organization wants to go in order to achieve its strategic objectives. The development of the BI roadmap takes into consideration not just the organization's priorities but also the information management gaps, along with industry practices, and the lessons learned from the development of the PoCs. Each phase of AIMS-BI identifies key areas that the organization should focus on and this culminates in a strategic BI roadmap that reflects a balanced portfolio of BI initiatives, a coherent implementation sequence, and provides a sound basis for ensuring that BI initiatives are aligned to organizational strategic priorities.

9

CREATING BUSINESS VALUE
FROM DATA ASSETS

[Organizations] most valuable asset, although not shown in the
financial statements, is data.

PwC[1]

Introduction

Data has become such an important asset and organizational resource
in the digital economy, that it is now being regarded as the new fuel or
the new raw material of the 21st century. But data as an asset has some
unique attributes that distinguish it from other traditional physical
assets. Specifically, unlike natural raw materials, data is not dimin-
ished when it is consumed. Indeed, the value of data assets increase in
direct relationship to the number of people who are able to make use
of the asset.

One of the important steps in building the commitment to Strategic
Business Intelligence (BI) is to be able to demonstrate the value of the
data assets. Although important, it is often not done as it is difficult
to quantify the value of the data asset. More recently, there has been a
focus on this and a number of options have been proposed. This issue
of measuring the value of data assets will be outlined in this chapter.

Edward Wilson made this perennial assertion:

We are drowning in information, while starving for wisdom. The world
henceforth will be run by synthesizers, people able to put together the
right information at the right time, think critically about it, and make
important choices wisely.

Wilson (1999)

---

[1] https://pwc.fr/fr/assets/files/pdf/2016/05/pwc_a4_data_governance_results.pdf.

Wilson's "*Synthesizers*" forecast the ascendancy of today's Analytics Competitors, organizations such as Google, Amazon, Capital One and Netflix that make widespread use of BI and data assets to create significant business value. Across industry sectors, *Synthesizers* manifest two key business attributes that have become significant enablers of their competitive advantage and strategic ambitions.

- Quality Data Assets: The distinctive quality of the data possessed by the organization that cannot be easily replicated by its competitors.
- Agility: The ability of the organization to rapidly sense and respond to volatile environmental changes by maximizing the use/leverage of its data assets.

Measuring Value of your Data Assets

While systematic methods and tools have emerged for assessing and measuring data quality, consensus on standardized methods for the valuation of data assets has continued to be elusive. In general, data quality needs to be examined, planned and managed within a larger Information Management context. The following definition of Information Management is a useful one: "a program that manages the people, processes, and technology in an enterprise toward the goal of maximizing the leverage, value, and investment in data and knowledge, while avoiding increased risk and cost due to data and knowledge misuse, poor handling, or exposure to regulatory scrutiny".[2] This definition underscores the importance to organizations of establishing a means of assessing the value of their data assets in order to provide relevant context to the efforts and resources allocated to data quality management activities. This is not, by any means, a trivial task. Information theorists have long struggled with the challenge of establishing a mechanism for the valuation of the intangible organizational data, information and knowledge assets. Gartner defines Infonomics[3] as follows:

---

[2] Ladley, J. (2005). Beyond the data warehouse: Plain English. DM Review, September.

[3] http://gartner.com/it-glossary/infonomics.

> Infonomics is the emerging discipline of managing and accounting for information with the same or similar rigor and formality as other traditional assets (e.g., financial, physical, intangible, human capital). Infonomics posits that information itself meets all the criteria of formal company assets, and, although not yet recognized by generally accepted accounting practices, increasingly, it is incumbent on organizations to behave as if it were to optimize information's ability to generate business value.

Infonomics is the emerging discipline of managing and accounting for information with the same or similar rigor and formality as other traditional assets and posits that information itself meets all the criteria of formal company assets. While not yet recognized by generally accepted accounting practices, increasingly, it is incumbent on organizations to behave as if it were to optimize information's ability to generate business value, in the same way that other more traditional physical assets are acquired, valued, accounted for and leveraged.

Unfortunately, while some companies recognize and account for the value of intangible assets, such as brands and intellectual property, relatively few have any sense of the value of their data assets. According to Gartner Research, 90% of surveyed executives list data as one of their most important competitive assets, but fewer than 10% of them actually quantify it.

Method of Information Value Assessment

Within the global Data ecosystem, analysts (e.g. McKinsey) estimate a combined realizable value of over $20 trillion for Open Data, Big Data, Digitization and IoT Data (Internet of Things). At the level of the individual firm, methods for estimating the value of data assets include:

1. **Cost (Historical Cost)**: This is the traditional cost accounting approach to valuing assets based on how much was originally paid to acquire the asset (purchase price and/or development cost).
2. **Market (Current Cash Equivalent)**: Using this method, an asset is valued based on how much other people or organizations are prepared to pay for it. One conceptual method for

this value assessment is to determine the market value of the business (i.e. share capital), then assess how much an independent third party (such as a potential buyer) would value the organization if it was offered without the historical information about its products, customers, staff and risk. Informal estimates suggest this drop in market value could range from more than 50% to less than 30%, depending on the information intensity of the organization (consider for instance, Amazon's market value without its data assets).

3. **Utility (Present Value)**: This method estimates the value of the data assets based on the net present value of expected future economic benefits. Theoretically, this is the best indicator of the value of data but it is often more practical to apply this method in the cost-benefit analysis and justification of discrete Analytics project initiatives rather than for assessing the overall value of the enterprise information assets.

We used the second method (market value) with several companies to develop theoretical estimates of their data assets. Figure 9.1 illustrates the computations for a hypothetical company on the local Jamaica Stock Exchange (JSE) Junior Market. Company X's business model is heavily dependent on data as a key business resource, so we estimate their data assets to be worth 25% of the market value.

This exercise helps organizations to put a tangible value to initiatives such as systematic data quality management to arrest the rate of information value depreciation. Even with conservative estimates

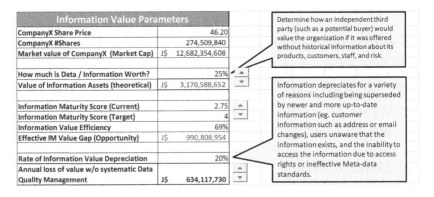

Figure 9.1   Estimating the value of the company's data assets.

of 20% or less of the business' market value, this hypothetical valuation provides an important point of reference that will help to do the following:

1. Increase Awareness: Increasing awareness of the value of data as an organizational asset, which may lead to commensurate attention being given to its management and leverage in comparison to more modestly valued physical assets.
2. Improve accountability: Measuring the value of data will give greater impetus to the institution of roles and responsibilities such as data stewardship/custodians.
3. Cost-justification of BI Initiatives: There is typically greater difficulty in cost-justifying BI projects relative to more conventional operational systems. An information valuation paradigm is much more appropriate for such systems.

Managing the Value of your Data Assets

Once organizations ascribe a business value to their data assets, it becomes much easier for Executive Management to appreciate and elevate the strategic importance of improved Data Governance practices because the loss of business value due to poor data quality and ineffective data use become quantifiable business outcomes rather than anecdotal narratives.

The components of such a systematic Data Governance program could include the following:

- Data Standards catalog & Metadata Management: Establish a Metadata catalog of all the key Data and Information Assets across the business to provide a centralized, searchable electronic repository of assets, not dissimilar to any well-managed financial assets register.
- Data Quality Management: Establish a formal Data Quality Management process for Enterprise Data, facilitated by an Enterprise Data Quality Platform that integrates all of the requisite functions, including profiling, cleansing, standardization and Data Quality Dashboard functions to monitor data quality metrics and support data governance initiatives (see Chapter 6).

- Establish Data Stewardship: Institutionalizing Data Stewardship by defining the necessary roles, procedures, support and accountability mechanisms to identify and empower Data Stewards to help formulate and oversee adherence to Data Quality standards and policies.
- Information Value Models/Metrics: Work on developing economic models for the value of information and opportunity costs of data quality in order to inform management on how to assure returns on investments in data assets.

Returning to Edward Wilson's prescient assertion, two decades hence, the *Synthesizers* that run the world of business and commerce today, are those that have accumulated enormous repositories of data assets coupled with distinctive analytic capabilities that cannot be readily reproduced by their competitors.

Benefits Realization Management (BRM)

Like any other business asset, estimating and ascribing a value to data assets helps organizations to determine the appropriateness of measures for managing and protecting the asset. However this activity alone does not provide a basis for realizing the future economic benefits from the utilization of the asset. Benefits Realization Management (BRM) is a collective set of processes, practices and tools that can help managers to increase the likelihood that benefits are realized from BI and other ICT-enabled initiatives.

BRM is a continuous process that includes investment decision-making using cost-benefit analysis, project management, implementation, monitoring and continuous adjustment. It is a disciplined approach that is based on the central tenets that technology alone cannot deliver business benefits, and benefits rarely happen completely according to plans or intent. Thus BRM prescribes a systematic process of management activities that consists of the following stages (Figure 9.2):

Figure 9.2   Stages of management activities.

Benefits Identification: At the inception of each project initiative, business benefits are clearly identified and quantified using cost-benefit analysis. A business manager is assigned as the owner of each benefit, with full responsibility for its realization. The collection of the planned benefits are usually captured and managed in a benefits register. In addition, a Benefits Realization Roadmap is sometimes developed to provide a visual illustration that shows when and how benefits are expected to be enabled for the business over the course of the project.

Benefits Analysis and Planning: Benefits are prioritized, and metrics are developed to allow each Benefit to be monitored and tracked throughout the project. It is important that the expected realization of Benefits is integrated into the overall program plan.

Benefits Delivery: This involves continuous monitoring of the project implementation, and maintaining and updating the Benefits register as the program progresses. The realization of benefits or any changes to the benefits expectations should be reported to the management team.

Benefits Transition/Sustainment: Once benefits are realized through the project, ongoing responsibility for maintaining the benefits should be handed over to operational management to continue to monitor benefits performance and ensure that the emergent results are continued. A Benefits Sustainment Plan can be established to identify risks, processes, measures and tools necessary to ensure the continued realization of the benefits.

Ultimately the implementation of BI and other ICT-enabled initiatives provide organizations with enhanced capabilities. However, for benefits realization to be effective and sustainable, business managers must assume activist responsibility for orchestrating the key business changes and processes necessary to take advantage of these capabilities to realize the benefits.

Over time, Organizations need to reassess their Information maturity capability to determine the impact of the BI initiatives within the organization. In Chapter 3, we had discussed two key measures in the Information maturity assessment namely *value creation* and *data usage quality*. By tracking these measures over progressive assessment cycles as they execute their BI Roadmap, business managers will have a qualitative and quantitative assessment of whether the BI Initiatives are delivering real business value for the organization.

Conclusion/Recommendations

The primary rationale for BI should be to realize maximum returns from data assets. Returns may take the form of increases in operational efficiency, employee productivity, time to market, sales and revenue as well as mitigating costs which may be realized as process failures, opportunity costs, scrap and rework costs and the failure to sense and act on business opportunities. Developing economic models for the value of information and opportunity costs of data quality can be demonstrated in a PoC but should be extended and institutionalized to provide the organization with systemic approaches to measurement, ranking and quantification of data/information value creation activities.

Epilogue: Lessons Learned

Think big and don't listen to people who tell you it can't be done.
Life's too short to think small.

Tim Ferriss

Small and Medium-Sized Enterprises (SMEs) must not be intimidated by the notion of becoming data-driven organizations, rather they should recognize the opportunity to become leaders in this space. They should not be stymied by the perception that it is extremely resource intensive to become data-driven. This books seeks to dispel the perception by providing a methodology, AMIS-BI, that SMEs can adopt and adapt, taking into account nuances that are specific to their own enterprises.

Critical Success Factors

There is a plethora of case studies that describe the effect that strategic BI initiatives have had on organizations and the areas in which these initiatives have been applied. These case studies identify a number of factors that have been critical to the success of the BI initiatives, many of which were supported by our own experiences working with SMEs.

Many organizations have invested significantly in BI initiatives without fully understanding and implementing the critical success factors; consequently they have not been able to reap the expected benefits. A part of the roadmap must include a plan for ensuring that the critical success factors will be in place to support the implementation of the BI initiatives. From the literature and our own experiences, we have compiled the following list of critical success factors SMEs must consider as they invest in BI initiatives:

1. The alignment of data-driven initiatives and strategic objectives.
2. Changing the mind-set of employees. Decision-making must be based on data, and not, as previously, on intuition. So move from a culture of intuition-based decision to one of data-driven decision-making.
3. Identifying a champion at the senior level – We have found that those organizations that have an influential champion are those that have had the most success applying AIMS-BI. The role of the senior level designated champion in ensuring stakeholder engagement throughout the process can not be underestimated.
4. Communicating with all stakeholders. Stakeholders must be kept up to date on the progress of AIMS-BI during its application. The champion has a critical role here.
5. Data quality. This is foundational to BI success. Therefore, unless the organization has previously done so, as part of the BI roadmap a formal data quality process must be developed to maintain the quality of the data.
6. Identifying the right team. A BI project is not an IT only initiative, it requires a mix of team members including business analysts, data analysts, BI analysts.

Based on our experience and feedback from applying AIMS-BI to organizations, this methodology is suited to SMEs as it includes a number of activities that are relevant to their needs but that have not been considered in the more traditional BI approaches. These activities include the following:

1. The IM assessment – This assessment has proved to be an extremely useful first step in identifying the state of strategic BI readiness of an organization as it helps to identify the areas

that need improvement if the organization is to maximize the benefits of its BI investment. There is a close alignment between the IM assessment areas and the critical success factors for BI implementation which means that the assessment is measuring areas key to the success of BI. We found that the self-evaluation is an important feature of this IM assessment as it makes the stakeholders more open to the findings than if an external assessor acting independently was to carry this out. The stakeholders felt that this step validated their own views on organizational weaknesses (e.g. data quality). The results of the Information Maturity Assessment form an important step for BI capability benchmarking and the results form an important input to the development of the BI roadmap.

2. Proof of Concepts (PoCs) and Prototypes. The PoCs and, more specifically, the development of the prototypes demonstrated to the executive management team and all key stakeholders the business value of advanced analytics, systematic approaches to better data quality management, and the agility of data as a service. The prototypes also helped stakeholders to better understand the process of implementing BI as a whole, and not just the analytics component, as well the factors that are critical to its success. All of this secured/reinforced executive commitment to strategic BI.

3. Engagement. Engaging the senior executives and other key stakeholders early in the process proved to be invaluable for getting the buy-in for the project. It was interesting to see the level of interest and commitment of the senior executives and all other key sponsors.

4. Agility. Deployment agility was enabled through the use of Open Source software. There are a number of benefits including reduced lead-time, cost, time-to-value and, importantly, increased opportunity for experimentation. The agile methodology of AIMS-BI helps to ensure that the BI initiatives are enterprise in scope, strategically aligned, executive-driven and portfolio-based, which are all key success factors for such initiatives.

Appendix: Case Studies

Academic Analytics for an Educational Institution

A leading higher educational institution in the Caribbean is faced with the challenge of how to get more value from its data and is considering investing in analytics. Senior management and key decision-makers have expressed their concern about the lack of access to clean data that are essential to their critical decision-making and they want to identify opportunities for the application of academic analytics.

AIMS-BI was applied to the academic institution

Business Needs	Our Approach	Client Results

• The institution wanted to identify academic analytics opportunities.
• They needed to identify their barriers to strategic Business Intelligence (BI) adoption.
	• The Information Management (IM) assessment was administered.
	• Low maturity scores for policy and measurement signaled clear gaps in formal data governance mechanisms and the minimal use of best practice behaviors such as data quality metrics and profiling/measurement.
	• The finding from IM assessment was corroborated by the qualitative comments recorded from the various user group interviews.
	• The main strategic objectives of the organization were also elicited. They were based on student experience, finance, efficiency and research.
	• A portfolio of initiatives was developed that included the development of a student life-cycle dashboard, the establishment of data stewardship, a research productivity dashboard and data quality management processes.
	• Senior management was asked to prioritize those Proof of concepts (PoCs).
	• The student life cycle was chosen as the prototype to be developed.
	• This initiative was considered to be critical as it aligned with two key strategic objectives:
	  • Improving academic and administrative process efficiency.
	  • Improving student experience.
	• The Knowledge Discovery and Data Mining (KDM) process model was used to develop this prototype.
	• A number of dashboards, that focused on application processing and student throughput were developed.
		• AIMS-BI is useful for educational institutions
		• AIMS-BI provides a systematic approach to academic analytics and in so doing can maximize the benefits analytics can provide.
		• The PoCs must be aligned with the strategic objectives of the institution.
		• Capability gaps that are essential for successful analytics are identified from the IM assessment, plans to address these become a part of the roadmap.
		• A significant amount of time and effort was spent to get the data from the form in the heterogeneous databases to a form suitable for the various modeling techniques. This highlighted the need for data standardization policies.
		• The primary output of this process is the roadmap; however, other important outputs are the prototypes that do not require much more effort for full deployment.
		• The student life cycle provides a basis for managing and optimizing the student experience by tracking students as they progress through the institution.

Data-Driven Credit Risk Models for a Financial Institution

A leading financial institution in the Caribbean is interested in analyzing payments data to determine if this data can provide a further understanding of customer behavior e.g. can the size and/or frequency of utility bill payments or retail transactions provide additional predictor variables for customer risk profiling? This institution is interested in reviewing its credit card scoring models to determine if payments data can be used to improve the quality of these models. They think reliable proxies from nontraditional sources could be used to determine the customers' ability to repay and willingness to pay. Six sources were identified as reliable: telecommunications providers, utilities, wholesale suppliers, retailers, government and the institutions' own previously overlooked data.

AIMS-BI was applied in the institution and data driven credit risk models were identified as one of the top priority PoCs that needed to be prototyped.

Business Needs

- The institution wants to consider other reliable and high-quality data they have access to with the aim of improving the credit card scoring models currently being used.

- These additional sources can be used as reliable proxies for customers' ability to repay.

- They need to build new credit card scoring models using variables from payments data.

Our Approach

- AIMS-BI was applied and in prioritizing the portfolio of PoCs, *improving credit risk models* was identified as a priority.

- The key stakeholders were interviewed and their concerns about the existing scoring models were discussed.

  - Included business analysts from payments and credit risk divisions

- Key decision-makers identified potential sources of data that could be used as proxies.

- This data was profiled to determine its quality and transformed so that it could be integrated into the scoring models.

- The predictive modeling technique (decision trees) was used to build profiles based on existing data.

- These prototype models were developed and verified with existing data.

Client Results

- These non-traditional sources proved to be important in determining the customers' ability to repay.

- Analysis of the payments data can provide a further understanding of customers.

- Payment data can be used to provide additional predictor variables to improve the performance of credit-risk scoring models.

- This data represents behavior which can be a better predictor than the salary/profit data reported by persons.

- Derived variables were created to build these models which require a good understanding of the domain knowledge and data.

- The institution recognized that they had issues with organizational metadata and data quality and this led to the inclusion of initiatives to address this being included in the BI roadmap.

- The prototype developed was near implementation ready so in the development of the BI roadmap, this was included as a short-term activity.

Transactors and Revolvers for a Financial Institution

A leading financial institution in the Caribbean needs to understand the credit card portfolio at the customer level by identifying the attributes associated with transactors (i.e. those that pay full amount of bill each month) and revolvers (i.e. those that pay a part of the amount with interest each month), and also identify the profiles of revolvers who are likely to become delinquent.

AIMS-BI was applied in the institution and this came out as one of the top-priority PoCs that needed to be prototyped.

Business Needs	Our Approach	Client Results
• The institution wants to determine whether customers bill payment patterns determine their propensity to either be a transactor or revolver and to determine how to make their transactors into revolvers yet ensure that revolvers will not become delinquent. • The institution needs to consider other reliable and high-quality data they have access to that can improve the understanding of the credit card portfolio. • Institutions want to be able to determine how to make their transactors into revolvers yet ensure that their revolvers are not likely to become delinquent.	• AIMS-BI was applied to this institution and in building the portfolio of PoCs, this need to understand the credit card portfolio was identified as one of the top priorities. • Further discussions were held with the affected decision-makers to identify potential sources of data that could be used as proxies. • This data was profiled to determine its quality and transformed so that it would be useful for integration in the scoring models. • Prototype models were developed and verified with existing data.	• Non-traditional sources proved to be important in determining the customers' ability to repay. • Credit card portfolio management was previously being done at the portfolio level this model supports, describing the portfolio at the customer level as each customer can be profiled. • The organization identified three groups – transactor, normal revolver and delinquent revolver. • The models can be used to determine the credit worthiness of a particular customer/potential customer whose credit risk is not yet known. • A great deal of time had to be spent in identifying the sources of the data needed to build this model. • The prototype developed from this was near implementation ready so in the development of the BI roadmap this could be included as a short-term activity. • The ability to identify customers' propensity to pay can personalize the interactions with them.

Market Basket Analysis for a Financial Institution

A leading financial institution in the Caribbean is focusing on building a sales culture to meet one of its strategic objectives of improving sales. The fact that some of its products have moderate or low penetration suggests that both the sales strategy and products should be reviewed. Additionally, there is an awareness of repeat customer take-up of related products, however, the evidence of how this functions is merely anecdotal. There is no systematic means of identifying related products or directing sales personnel to offer product bundles.

AIMS-BI was used in the institution and this came up as one of the most important PoCs that needed to be demonstrated to the stakeholders.

Business Needs

- The focus of this customer analytics initiative was to improve marketing strategies.
- Maximize the customer value to the organization by cross-selling/upselling various products to existing customers.
- This will ultimately contribute to the bank's revenue targets by improving the efficiency of sales initiatives

Our Approach

- AIMS-BI was applied to this institution and this initiative was included in the portfolio of PoCs.
- The business leader and business analyst were interviewed to get a better business understanding.
- To improve the success rate of current targeted marketing campaigns, market basket analysis was employed as a customer analytic technique.
- This technique uses association rule mining to identify the products that customers currently purchase together, which can be used to identify bundles (i.e. those products that go well together) and therefore that should be marketed accordingly.
- Customers don't necessarily buy financial products all at one time, therefore a basket contains products bought over time.
- Sequential rule mining was used as it shows not only which products were bought together but also the sequence in which they were bought.
- Concept hierarchies for the domain were developed to enable analysis at different levels of granularity.
- Numeric variables were discretized in consultation with financial business analysts who provided the linguistic terms used to describe each of the data ranges (e.g. age values were discretized to young, middle-aged, etc.).

Client Results

- Both association rules and sequential mining help to increase the effectiveness of sales campaign management and targeting processes.
- The concept hierarchies developed were extremely useful in classifying products into subgroups which were then used in the development of the models.
- The inclusion of demographic and product data together in a basket was novel and facilitates the discovery of multidimensional rules and frequent patterns in buying products.
- The data preparation phase is reliant on the knowledge and experience of the data mining analysts and importantly their understanding of the business objectives and the corresponding data required.
- The prototype developed was near implementation ready so this could be included as a short-term activity in the development of the BI roadmap.

Glossary

Agility: A methodology that promotes regular interactions amongst stakeholders, building prototypes and responsiveness to change.

AIMS-BI: Agile Integrated Methodology for Strategic Business Intelligence.

Analytical Hierarchical Processing (AHP): A Multi-Criteria Decision-Making technique that reduces complex decisions to a set of evaluation criteria, and a set of alternative options from which the best decision is to be made.

Analytics Competitors: Organizations that improve performance through the application of data analytics to their business processes.

Business Intelligence: Business Intelligence (BI) can be described as a set of techniques and tools for the acquisition and transformation of raw data into meaningful and useful information/knowledge for business analysis purposes.

Business Intelligence Competency Centre (BICC): A team of people that develop the overall strategic plan and priorities for BI.

Capability Gaps: Assess the current capabilities of the enterprise and identify the gaps that prevent it from meeting business needs and achieving desired outcomes.

Case Study: An evaluation method in Design Science research which entails studying the designed artifact (i.e. methodology) in depth in a business environment.

Corporate Data Warehouse: A central storage system for enterprise-wide data.

Critical Success Factors: Capabilities or circumstances necessary to enable a positive outcome for a business program or a strategy.

Cross-Industry Standard Process for Data Mining (CRISP-DM): A structured approach for implementing a data mining project.

Data as a Service (DaaS): A platform for data integration and management on a Cloud.

Data Assets: Data that is expected to generate future revenues.

Network Data Delivery Services (NDDS): NDDS provides transparent network connectivity and data ubiquity to a set of processes possibly running in different machines.

Data Standards Cataloging: Data standards are the rules by which data are described and recorded. In order to share, exchange and understand data, the format as well as the meaning must be standardized.

Data Stewardship: Data stewardship is the management and oversight of an organization's data assets according to established data governance practices.

Data Virtualization: Data virtualization integrates data from disparate sources, locations and formats, without replicating the data, to create a single "virtual" data layer that delivers unified data services to support multiple applications and users.

Design Science Research Methodology (DSR): A set of guidelines for the development and evaluation of Information, Communication and Technology (ICT) artifacts to address real-world problems.

Enterprise Information Management (EIM): Enterprise information management (EIM) is a set of business processes, disciplines and practices used to manage the information created from an organization's data as an enterprise asset. EIM is an integrative discipline for structuring, describing and governing information assets across organizational and technological boundaries to improve efficiency, promote transparency and enable business insight – Gartner.

Extraction Transformation and Loading (ETL): Extract, transform and load (ETL) is the process of integrating data from multiple, typically disparate, sources and bringing them together into one central location.

IBM-DGC Maturity Model (DGCMM): A model developed to ensure consistency and quality control in governance through proven business technologies, collaborative methods and best practices.

Information Management (IM) Maturity Model: A model that provides a standardized tool for consistent point-in-time assessment of the maturity of overall Information Management (IM) capabilities within an organization.

Information Management (IM) Maturity Assessment: Assesses the maturity levels for various organizational aspects related to Information Management and thus provides a benchmark for future assessments.

Key Performance Indicators (KPIs): A set of quantifiable measures that a company uses to gauge its performance over time.

Knowledge Discovery and Data Mining (KDDM) Process Model: A model that organizes Knowledge Discovery and Data Mining (KDDM) projects within a common framework. This helps organizations to understand the Knowledge Discovery process and to provide a road map to follow while planning and carrying out the projects.

Enterprise Metadata Management (EMM): The business discipline for managing the metadata about the information assets of the organization. Metadata is "information that describes various facets of an information asset to improve its usability throughout its life cycle." (Gartner).

Maturity Model: A tool that helps management determine the current effectiveness of a process and supports identifying the capabilities they need to acquire next in order to improve performance e.g. CMMI, OPM3.

MIKE2.0 IM QuickScan Tool (Methodology for an Integrated Knowledge Environment): An open source methodology for EIM that provides a framework for information development.

Multi-Criteria Decision-Making (MCDM): A branch of operational research dealing with finding optimal results in complex scenarios including various indicators, conflicting objectives and criteria.

Organizational Capabilities: An organizational capability is a company's ability to manage resources, such as employees, effectively to gain an advantage over competitors.

Proof of Concepts (PoCs): It is a realization of a certain method or idea in order to demonstrate its feasibility, or a demonstration in principle with the aim of verifying that some concept or theory has practical potential. A PoC is usually small and may or may not be complete.

Prototyping: A draft version of a solution that allows for the exploration of the solutions and demonstrates the intention behind the solution before investing time and money into its full-blown development.

Return on Investment (ROI): A financial ratio used to calculate the benefit of the investment in relation to the investment cost.

Semi-Structured Interviews: A meeting in which the interviewer does not strictly follow a formalized list of questions. The questions are open-ended.

SMEs: SMEs are small and medium-sized enterprises that are typically classified according to employee count and/or annual revenues. While there is no universal classification, what is not disputed is that in most economies they account for the majority of enterprises, contribute considerably to GDP, export and employment. They produce a significant portion of the private sector output.

Strategic Analytics: Detailed, data-driven, analyses supporting outcomes of strategic importance for a company.

Strategic BI Roadmap: Describes a proposed path of Strategic BI progression to meet the implementation of a delivery strategy. It reflects a balanced portfolio of BI initiatives and a coherent implementation sequence, and provides a sound basis for ensuring that BI initiatives are aligned to organizational strategic priorities.

Bibliography

Aberdeen-Group. (2011). Agile BI: Complementing traditional BI to address the shrinking decision window. Retrieved from http://montage.co.nz/assets/Brochures/Aberdeen-Agile-BI.pdf

Anderson-Lehman, R., Watson, H. J., Wixom, B. H., & Hoffer, J. A. (2004). Continental airlines flies high with real-time business intelligence. *MIS Quarterly Executive*, 3(4), 163–176.

Apte, C., Liu, B., Pednault, E., & Smyth, P. (2002). Business applications of data mining. *Communications of the ACM*, 45(8), 49–53.

Ariyachandra, T. & Watson, H. J. (2010). Key organizational factors in data warehouse architecture selection. *Decision Support Systems*, 49(2), 200–212.

Becker, J., Knackstedt, R., & Pöppelbuß, J. (2009). Developing maturity models for IT management. *Business and Information Systems Engineering*, 1(3), 213–222.

Bhambri, V. (2011). Application of data mining in banking sector. *International Journal of Computer Science and Technology*, 2(2), 199–202.

Breslin, M. (2004). Data warehousing battle of the giants. *Business Intelligence Journal*, 9(1), 6–20.

Brown, D. H. & Lockett, N. (2004). Potential of critical e-applications for engaging SMEs in e-business: A provider perspective. *European Journal of Information Systems*, 13(1), 21–34.

Chandler, N., Hostmann, B., Rayner, N., & Herschel, G. (2015). Gartner's business analytics framework. Gartner Inc.

Chapman, P., Clinton, J., Kerber, R., Khabaza, T., Reinartz, T., Shearer, C., & Wirth, R. (2000). CRISP-DM 1.0.

Chen, H., Chiang, R. H. L., & Storey, V. C. (2012). Business intelligence and analytics: From big data to big impact. *Management Information Systems Quarterly*, 36(4), 1165–1188.

Cios, K. J., Teresinska, A., Konieczna, S., Potocka, J., & Sharma, S. (2000). Diagnosing myocardial perfusion from PECT bull's-eye maps-A knowledge discovery approach. *IEEE Engineering in Medicine and Biology Magazine*, 19(4), 17–25.

Cockburn, A. & Highsmith, J. (2001). Agile software development, the people factor. *Computer*, 34(11), 131–133.

Cooper, B., Watson, H., Wixom, B., & Goodhue, D. (2000). Data warehousing supports corporate strategy at first American corporation. *MIS Quarterly*, 24(4), 547–567.

Davenport, T. H. & Harris, J. G. (2007). *Competing on Analytics: The New Science of Winning*. Boston, MA: Harvard Business School.

De Bruin, T., Freeze, R., Kaulkarni, U., & Rosemann, M. (2005). Understanding the main phases of developing a maturity assessment model. *Paper Presented at the 16th Australasian Conference on Information Systems (ACIS)*, Australia, New South Wales, Sydney.

Demirkan, H. & Delen, D. (2013). Leveraging the capabilities of service-oriented decision support systems: Putting analytics and big data in cloud. *Decision Support Systems*, 55(1), 412–421.

Eck, A., Keidel, S., Uebernickel, F., Schneider, T., & Brenner, W. (2014). Not all information systems are created equal: Exploring IT resources for agile systems delivery.

Elzinga, J., Horak, T., Lee, C.-Y., & Bruner, C. (1995). Business process management: Survey and methodology. *IEEE Transactions on Engineering Management*, 42(2), 119–128.

Evelson, B. (2011). *Trends 2011 and Beyond: Business Intelligence*, Vol. 31. Cambridge MA: Forrester Research, Inc.

Evelson, B. (2014). The Forrester Wave™: Agile business intelligence platforms, Q3 2014. Forrester Research Inc.

Fayyad, U., Piatetsky-Shapiro, G., & Smyth, P. (1996). From data mining to knowledge discovery in databases. *AI Magazine*, 17(3), 37–54.

Gregor, S. & Hevner, A. R. (2013). Positioning and presenting design science research for maximum impact. *MIS Quarterly*, 37(2), 337–356.

Hannula, M. & Pirttimaki, V. (2003). Business intelligence empirical study on the top 50 Finnish companies. *Journal of American Academy of Business*, 2(2), 593–599.

Hevner, A. R., March, S. T., Park, J., & Ram, S. (2004). Design science in information systems research. *MIS Quarterly*, 28(1), 75–105.

Highsmith, J. (2009). *Agile Project Management: Creating Innovative Products*. London, UK: Pearson Education.

Hostmann, B., Rayner, N., & Friedman, T. (2006). *Gartner's Business Intelligence and Performance Management Framework*. Stamford, CT: Gartner.

IBM. (2007). *The IBM Data Governance Council Maturity Model: Building a Roadmap for Effective Data Governance*. IBM Software Group. Retrieved from https://studylib.net/doc/8219376/the-ibm-data-governance-council-maturity-model--building-a

Inmon, W.H. (2005). *Building the Data Warehouse*. New York: John Wiley & Sons.

Jacobs, A. (2009). The pathologies of big data. *Communications of the ACM*, 52(8), 36–44.

Jourdan, Z., Rainer, R. K., & Marshall, T. E. (2008). Business intelligence: An analysis of the literature. *Information Systems Management*, 25(2), 121–131.

Jukic, N. (2006). Modeling strategies and alternatives for data warehousing projects. *Communications of the ACM*, 49(4), 83–88.

Katal, A., Wazid, M., & Goudar, R. H. (2013, August). Big data: Issues, challenges, tools and good practices. *2013 Sixth International Conference on Contemporary Computing (IC3)*, Noida, New Delhi (pp. 404–409). IEEE.

Kimball, R. & Ross, M. (2011). *The Data Warehouse Toolkit: The Complete Guide to Dimensional Modeling*. New York: John Wiley & Sons.

Knabke, T. & Olbrich, S. (2013). Understanding information system agility—the example of business intelligence. *Paper Presented at the 46th Hawaii International Conference on System Sciences*, Hawaii.

Kotelnikov, V. (2007). Small and medium enterprises and ICT, United Nations Development Program-Asia Pacific Development Information Program. Asian and Pacific Training Center for Information and Communication Technology for Development.

Kurgan, L. A. & Musilek, P. (2006). A survey of knowledge discovery and data mining process models. *The Knowledge Engineering Review*, 21(1), 1–24.

Lee, Y. & Koza, K. A. (2006). Investigating the effect of website quality on e-business Success: An Analytic Hierarchy Process (AHP) approach. *Decision Support Systems*, 42, 1383–1401.

Loveman, G. (2003). Diamonds in the data mine. *Harvard Business Review*, 81(5), 109–113.

Mansingh, G., Osei-Bryson, K.-M., & Asnani, M. (2015). Exploring the antecedents of the quality of life of patients with sickle cell disease: Using a knowledge discovery and data mining process model based framework. *Health Systems: Palgrave McMillan,* 5(1), 52–65.

Mansingh, G., Osei-Bryson, K.-M., & Reichgelt, H. (2010). Using ontologies to facilitate post-processing of association rules by domain experts. *Information Sciences*, 181(3), 419–434.

Mansingh, G. & Rao, L. (2014). Enhancing the decision making process: An ontology based approach. *Paper Presented at the International Conference on Information Resources Management (Conf-IRM)*, Ho Chi Minh City, Vietnam.

Mansingh, G., Rao, L., Osei-Bryson, K.-M., & Mills, A. (2015). Profiling internet banking users: A knowledge discovery in data mining process model based approach. *Information Systems Frontiers*, 17(1), 193–215.

March, S. T. & Smith, G. F. (1995). Design and natural science research on information technology. *Decision Support Systems*, 15(4), 251–266.

Mariscal, G., Marban, O., & Fernandez, C. (2010). A survey of data mining and knowledge discovery process models and methodologies. *The Knowledge Engineering Review*, 25(2), 137–166.

Melon, M. G., Beltran, P. A., & Cruz, M. C. G. (2008). An AHP-based evaluation procedure for innovative educational projects: A face-to-face vs. computer-mediated case study. *Omega*, 36(5), 754–765.

Meredith, R., Remington, S., O'Donnell, P., & Sharma, N. (2012). Organisational transformation through Business Intelligence: Theory, the vendor perspective and a research agenda. *Journal of Decision Systems*, 21(3), 187–201.

Mettler, T. (2009). A design science research perspective on maturity models in information systems tech. report BE IWI/HNE/03: Universität St. Gallen.

Moin, K. I. & Ahmed, Q. B. (2012). Use of data mining in banking. *International Journal of Engineering Research and Applications*, 2(2), 738–742.

Mooney, J., Beath, C., Fitzgerald, G., Ross, J., & Weill, P. (2003). Managing information technology for strategic flexibility and agility: Rethinking conceptual models, architecture, development, and governance. *Paper Presented at the International Conference on Information Systems (ICIS)*, Seattle, Washington.

Muntean, M. & Surcel, T. (2013). Agile BI–the future of BI. *Revista Informatica Economică*, 17(3), 114–124.

Negash, S. (2004). Business intelligence. *Communications of the Association for Information Systems*, 13, 177–195.

Negash, S. & Gray, P. (2008). Business intelligence. In *Handbook on Decision Support Systems*, Vol. 2, pp. 175–193. Berlin, Heidelberg: Springer.

Ngai, E. W. T. (2003). Selection of web sites for online advertising using the AHP. *Information and Management*, 40, 1–10.

Olson, D. L., Dursun D., & Yanyan M. (2012). Comparative analysis of data mining methods for bankruptcy prediction. *Decision Support Systems*, 52(2), 464–473.

Osei-Bryson, K. M., Mansingh, G., & Rao, L. (Eds.). (2014). *Knowledge Management for Development: Domains, Strategies and Technologies for Developing Countries*, Vol. 35. Springer Science & Business Media.

Overby, E., Bharadwaj, A., & Sambamurthy, V. (2006). Enterprise agility and the enabling role of information technology. *European Journal of Information Systems*, 15(2), 120–131.

Paranape-Voditel, P. & Deshpande, U. (2013). A stock market portfolio recommender system based on association rule mining. *Applied Soft Computing*, 13, 1055–1063.

Popovič, A., Hackney, R., Coelho, P. S., & Jaklič, J. (2012). Towards business intelligence systems success: Effects of maturity and culture on analytical decision making. *Decision Support Systems*, 54, 729–739.

Rouse, W. B. (2007). Agile information systems for agile decision making. *Agile Information Systems*, KC DeSouza, Editor, Elsevier, New York, 16–30.

Rygielski, C., Jyun-Cheng, W., & Yen, D. C. (2002). Data mining techniques for customer relationship management. *Technology in Society*, 24, 483–502.

Saaty, T. (1980). *The Analytic Hierarchy Process: Planning, Priority Setting, Resource Allocation*. New York: McGraw-Hill.

Sambamurthy, V., Bharadwaj, A., & Grover, V. (2003). Shaping agility through digital options: Reconceptualizing the role of information technology in contemporary firms. *MIS Quarterly*, 27, 237–263.

Sein, M. K., Henfridsson, O., Purao, S., Rossi, M., & Lindgren, R. (2011). Action design research. *MIS Quarterly*, 35, 37–56.

Sharma, S. & Osei-Bryson, K.-M. (2010). Toward an integrated knowledge discovery and data mining process model. *The Knowledge Engineering Review*, 25(1), 49–67.

Sharma, S., Osei-Bryson, K.-M., & Kasper, G. M. (2012). Evaluation of an integrated knowledge discovery and data mining process model. *Expert Systems with Applications*, 39, 11335–11348.

Steinmueller, W. E. (2001). ICTs and the possibilities for leapfrogging by developing countries. *International Labour Review*, 140(2), 193–210.

Thompson, S. & Brown, D. (2008). Change agents intervention in e-business adoption by SMEs: evidence from a developing country. *AMCIS 2008 Proceedings*, Paper# 242.

Thomsen, C. & Pedersen, T. B. (2009). A survey of open source tools for business intelligence. *International Journal of Data Warehousing and Mining (IJDWM)*, 5(3), 56–75.

Trkman, P., McCormack, K., Valadares de Oliveira, M. P., & Ladeira, M. B. (2010). The impact of business analytics on supply chain performance. *Decision Support Systems*, 49, 318–327.

Van der Lans, R. (2012). *Data Virtualization for Business Intelligence Systems: Revolutionizing Data Integration for Data Warehouses*. Waltham, MA: Elsevier.

van Steenbergen, M., Bos, R., Brinkkemper, S., van de Weerd, I., & Bekkers, W. (2010). The design of focus area maturity models. In: Winter, R., Zhao, J. L., Aier, S. (eds.) *Global Perspectives on Design Science Research*. DESRIST 2010. Lecture Notes in Computer Science, Vol. 6105. Berlin, Heidelberg: Springer.

Watson, H. J. (2009). Tutorial: business intelligence-past, present, and future. *Communications of the Association for Information Systems*, 25(1), 39.

Williams, S. & Williams, N. (2006). *The Profit Impact of Business Intelligence*. San Francisco, CA: Morgan Kaufmann.

Watson, H. J. & Wixom, B. H. (2007). The current state of business intelligence. *Computer*, 40(9), 96–99.

Watson, H. J., Fuller, C., & Ariyachandra, T. (2004). Data warehouse governance: Best practices at blue cross and blue shield of North Carolina. *Decision Support Systems*, 38(3), 435–450.

Wilson, E. O. (1999). *Consilience: The Unity of Knowledge*, Vol. 31. New York: Vintage.

Wilson, N., Summers, B., & Hope, R. (2000). Using payment behaviour data for credit risk modelling. *International Journal of the Economics of Business*, 7(3), 333–346.

Witter, M. & Kirton, C. (1990). The informal economy in Jamaica: Some empirical exercises (No. 36). Institute of Social and Economic Research, The University of the West Indies.

Index

For Product Safety Concerns and Information please contact our EU
representative GPSR@taylorandfrancis.com Taylor & Francis Verlag GmbH,
Kaufingerstraße 24, 80331 München, Germany

Printed and bound by CPI Group (UK) Ltd, Croydon, CR0 4YY
08/05/2025
01864338-0004